Adventure Guide to the

Catskills &
Adirondacks

Wilbur H. Morrison

D0167011

HUNTER
PUBLISHING INC

Hunter Publishing, Inc.
300 Raritan Center Parkway
Edison NJ 08818
(908) 225 1900
Fax (908) 417 0482

ISBN 1-55650-681-3

© 1995 Wilbur H. Morrison

Maps: Kim André

Cover: Adirondack Lake/*Superstock*

For Frank Morrison

Contents

List of Maps

Introduction

I was born in Plattsburgh, New York in 1915 and grew up in the foothills of the Adirondacks. I began to fish when I was 10 years old and to hunt two years later with my cousin Frank Morrison. This was a marvelous country in which to grow up, particularly for someone like me who has always loved the outdoors. The winters, which can be severe, with temperatures in Plattsburgh frequently below 30° for days, sometimes weeks at a time, rarely restricted my activities. I loved to skate, ski and toboggan in winter over vast snow-covered landscapes with seldom more than a dozen people near me. In spring, I eagerly awaited the start of the trout season, although the wily brook trout often proved elusive. But I loved to tramp along lonely streams with Frank and sneak up on a beaver pond to catch the busy animals at work or play. I was rarely successful, and a slap on the water by a beaver's tail gave evidence they had spotted me. In the fall, Frank and I tramped the woods, hunting mostly for cottontail rabbits and partridges. A neighbor let us borrow his bloodhound for most of these hunting trips, and I can still hear Sport's exciting baying when he found a hot trail. We never found pheasants and only an occasional snowshoe rabbit. There were ducks, but they were not plentiful. Neither of us had any interest in hunting deer or bear.

Frank and I, with other friends, climbed all the highest peaks. Much later Frank became a "46er," meaning he had climbed all the peaks. I can still vividly recall my first trip up Whiteface, with the magnificent 100-mile view and the penetrating cold of the sharp wind. The highest peak, Marcy, took longer to climb and the view from its summit was spectacular, with that lovely little body of water so aptly named Lake Tear Of The Clouds, where the Hudson River starts its trickle down the mountainside to become a mighty river.

I left Plattsburgh in the winter of 1937 and, except for visits, I have never lived there again. I eventually moved to California, where I live today.

I returned to the Adirondacks and the Catskills in 1994 to renew my acquaintance with the region, finding it vastly changed from the days of my youth, but still incredibly magnificent. Some of the land shows the ravages of millions of tourists, but by and large it has withstood this onslaught of humanity with casual dignity. Actually, I found the animal population much increased, and the fishing in most places vastly improved since my youth. Some lakes, possibly due to acid rain, have become so acidic that fish no longer can live in them. Flowing streams usually offer better prospects.

The Adirondacks and Catskills offer unparalled opportunities to relax or to be more physically active in a great variety of activities. Their proximity to highly-populated urban areas is not apparent. It is only 169 miles from Albany to Plattsburgh, 317 miles from New York, 334 miles from Boston, and 414 miles from Philadelphia. Each of these cities is less than a day's drive to the upper extensions of the Adirondacks via modern expressways.

Two words of caution. First, do not enter wilderness areas alone. You could easily lose your life due to an accident or become lost in that bewildering maze of shrubbery and trees. I personally will not drink water from streams or lakes even in the high peaks areas because of possible pollution. Where the water is safe to drink, a sign will tell you so. Even in the deep wilderness areas, you never know what or who has polluted the water. Play it safe and you'll enjoy your trip to the Adirondacks and Catskills to the fullest.

In the section on The Changing Seasons I've tried to outline the advantages and disadvantages of each month of the year. Select the month that most closely parallels the activities you intend to participate in.

I've traveled to most parts of the world and I have been to all states except Alaska. Each place has much to offer, but I rank the Adirondacks and the Catskills two of the most beautiful and exciting places I've ever known. If you're visiting them for the first time, I sincerely believe you will agree.

Wilbur H. Morrison
Fallbrook, CA

The
Adirondacks

History

The Adirondack Mountains are part of the Canadian Shield that extends to the Arctic Ocean on either side of the Hudson's Bay. A mass of granite, formed when the earth was born some 3.6 billion years ago, the "shield" spreads north, east and west. The Adirondacks are about 1.1 billion years old. They were worn down to their present size as the fourth glacier of the Great Ice Age a million or so years ago spread snow and ice to a depth of 10,000 feet across the Adirondacks, eroding their peaks and hollowing deep valleys. Then the earth began slowly warming up and the glacier retreated. It had spread across New England and into the Atlantic Ocean beyond Long Island, New York. As the ice and snow melted, the valleys were filled with water. The Lake George Depression, which had been scoured out by the moving glaciers, first spread beyond its present banks, then receded to its modern dimensions.

In 1570 the Cayuga, Mohawk, Oneida, Onondaga and Seneca tribes controlled the water routes in the Northeast and dominated trading between Indian tribes. That year they formed the Confederation of Five Nations. By 1700, they were strong enough to control the balance of power between the French and the British.

Samuel de Champlain, leader of the group of French and Indians who discovered Lake Champlain in 1609. (Prints Division, New York Public Library)

Except for hunting parties of Abenakis and Iroquois, the Indians never settled in the Adirondacks. The Mohawks, one of the Five Nations in Central New York, and the Algonquins in Canada both laid claim to the region but neither tribe was interested in living year-round in a land whose winters could be severe and growing basic crops was a doubtful enterprise. The Iroquois traveled over thousands of square miles in upstate New York, but they numbered only a few thousand by the end of the 17th Century. The Algonquin tribes were even smaller. Indians of that era readily succumbed to disease and suffered heavy losses in their constant battles with one another.

Although the exact date is unknown, Samuel de Champlain entered the lake that now bears his name in 1609. There is reason to believe that it was in July when he became the first white man to explore the lake, along with 11 companions and a war party of Huron, Montagnais and Algonquin Indians. The lake was well known to Indians in the region. Hurons and Algonquins headed uplake to make war on their traditional enemies, the Iroquois, while warriors of the Five Nations moved downlake in their large bark canoes. During a fateful encounter on a promontory at the head of the lake later known as Ticonderoga, Champlain's party met a band of Iroquois and he fired on them with his arquebus. Two of its four shells killed two Iroquois chiefs. A companion then fired and Champlain reloaded and fired again. The Iroquois were routed and a dozen captured. The encounter, out of all proportion to its significance at the time, created an animosity against the

Samuel de Champlain and his party attacked by Iroquoian warriors at Ticonderoga in 1609. (Rare Books Division, New York Public Library)

French among the Iroquois that had enormous repurcussions. Later on, when Indian tribes chose up sides in the wars between the French and the British and later with the colonists, they became British allies.

Champlain had come to Canada to try and revive the French settlement at Montreal, but he never returned to the lake which bears his name. He was warm in its praise, saying there were "a number of beautiful islands filled with fine woods and prairies."

French explorer Jacques Cartier had admired the mountains later known as the Adirondacks from afar on October 2, 1536, gazing up at them from an Indian village near what is now Montreal. Originally it was believed they were named for a tribe of Indians who had once hunted there. Actually Adirondack is not the name of a single tribe but an insult used to describe various groups. At one time the Algonquins controlled the Adirondacks but were driven out by the Iroquois. The word "Adirondack" is an Iroquoian word.

Mohawk chief depicted in 1710. His totem, the Bear, is shown at right.
(Library of Congress)

Some historians believe it was first used against the Algonquins because they were forced to live on tree buds and bark during severe winters. J. B. Hewitt of the Smithsonian Institution contends that Adirondack was derived from the language of the Indians who lived on the lower St. Lawrence River in the early 1500s and meant "They of the Great Rocks." He contends that the Iroquois, in adding the word to their language, gave it the new meaning of "They Who Eat Trees." Early Dutch traders, who developed a vocabulary of Mohawk words, claimed the word, spelled by them "adirondacke," meant Frenchmen and Englishmen. Cartier never got closer than 70 miles from the Adirondacks. He was told by the Indians that it was a mountainous terrain and an unexplored wilderness of lakes, mountains and delightful plains.

Lake Champlain, extending for 107 miles from Whitehall in New York State to Missisquoi Bay in Canada, is one of the loveliest bodies of water in the world. It forms the eastern boundary of Adirondack Park, but it is not part of it. Even today its approximately 80 islands are richly covered with evergreens. The lake is long and narrow except where it broadens to 12 miles between Burlington, Vermont and the New York shore.

Although Champlain never returned to the lake in later years, it soon became a pathway for invasion both from the north and the south. For more than 200 years fleets periodically fought for control of Lake Champlain because it was a natural military route. With roads almost non-existent in colonial times, the movement of men and supplies was far more rapid and efficient by water than by land. Strategically located, particularly during the early years of the United States, Lake Champlain, Lake George and the Hudson River offered the best line of communication from Canada to the heart of the new republic. Their control, therefore, was vital to the success of any military campaign.

Less than two months after Samuel de Champlain visited the lake that now bears his name, Henry Hudson's "Half Moon" sailed up the Hudson River in September 1609 beyond present-day Albany and he spied the Catskills and the Adirondacks from afar.

Most of the time Lake Champlain is a placid body of water, and perhaps that's all Champlain encountered during his brief journey up the lake. But others since have learned, often to their sorrow, that the lake can be contrary. Sometimes the sapphire blue water is serene. But changes come quickly and, with strong winds out of the north and northwest, it becomes a treacherous waterway for those who are not familiar with its violent whims.

The rushing waters that pour into it from the mountains on each side raise the lake's level, forcing it to empty into the Richelieu River through foaming rapids and finally into the St. Lawrence River near Montreal. At its deepest point, the lake is almost 400 feet deep, forming a trough between the Adirondack Mountains to the west and the far peaks of the Green Mountains of Vermont to the east.

The Adirondack region was slow to develop during the 170 years after its discovery by white people. The Indians proved hostile and even Jesuit missionaries were routinely tortured after they tried to Christianize the Indians. Trappers from Montreal and Fort George (Albany) traveled the region and found it teeming with wildlife. In the middle of the 18th Century a few hardy pioneers settled on the fringes of the Adirondacks. Their lives were made miserable by Indian raids and fighting between the British and French, then between British and American rebels seeking independence from Great Britain.

The southern boundary of the Adirondacks is about 200 miles north of New York City, and approximately 50 miles north of Albany. These relatively short distances should have brought about a much earlier settlement of the region, but it was not even seriously explored until the 1830s. Much of the Far West was better known than the Adirondacks, which were given that name in 1837. But after that, and throughout the remainder of the 19th Century, hotels and hunting lodges filled the Adirondacks and swarms of people descended upon the region during the summer months. It has been popular ever since.

What is now the Adirondack State Park totals 5,000 square miles. It is approximately the size of Connecticut, and forms a rectangle. Although much of it is wilderness, you can drive across the park in almost any direction in less than three hours. No area within the park is more than 10 miles from some sort of road. The southeastern section is centered at Lake George and is noted for its low hills and its lovely lakes.

While the French chose to expand the territory of "New France" westward instead of to the south, the Dutch established a trading post made of logs at a site they referred to as Fort Nassau, where present-day Albany now stands. Mohawk, and later Oneida Indians, quickly realized they could trade furs there for such valuable commodities as muskets.

An English group meanwhile landed in the *Mayflower* under Captain Christopher Jones on December 20, 1620, to establish a colony of religious fanatics at Plymouth in present-day Massachusetts. Although half of the colonists died that first winter, the survivors prospered in this new land and began to expand far beyond their original area. The French were more interested in the fur trade than in colonization so, by the time the Pilgrims landed at Plymouth, there were only 50 French inhabitants in Quebec.

England, at war with France in 1629, had sent a fleet under David Kirks up the St. Lawrence and accepted the surrender of Quebec and all of New France. Three years later the British gave the territory back to France.

Cardinal Richelieu now was given responsibility for the administration of New France, although Champlain was in charge on the local level. The Jesuits sent representatives of their order to Quebec to stamp out heresy and redeem New France's heathen souls. Champlain, a devout man, cooperated fully but he died in 1635. He was replaced by Charles Hualt de Montagny, who encouraged the westward expansion of Jesuit missions.

Montagny was a soldier of limited talents and was given only a few troops to enforce the laws in his vast new world. Despite the intense hostility of the Iroquois, now being heavily armed by the Dutch at their trading post in Albany in exchange for furs, only those Indians who had converted to Christianity in "New France" were permitted to purchase guns. Now the French faced the members of the Five Nations who had vowed to exterminate the Algonquins and Hurons, along with their French allies.

Fur-bearing animals in the Adirondacks declined drastically as the Iroquois systematically reduced their numbers. Now the Iroquois routinely made raids into Canada, where the supply seemed inexhaustible. Armed with muskets, Iroquois war parties moved north through Lake Champlain and the local Indians were almost literally wiped out. Few of them had firearms and they were nearly defenseless. They fought back with bows and arrows. Each summer this wholesale slaughter went on and the Iroquois engaged in cannibalistic feasts on their age-old enemies.

Intermittent periods of peace and war governed the Lake Champlain area for a number of years. The Iroquois mounted their most vicious attack when all Five Nations sent 1,500 warriors on August 5, 1689, to Lachine, five miles above Montreal, and literally destroyed it. Survivors told of Iroquois who killed and dined on their captives.

The following year a colonial struggle broke out again between France and Great Britain that endured, despite intermittent truces, for 70 years. The Lake Champlain-Lake George valley again erupted into savage attacks with dreary repetition.

The English colonies had fought the French with little assistance from the mother country, except for some impractical advice that cost them dearly. For the most part the colonists were disillusioned by the peace treaty that left them in physical and financial ruin.

The Iroquois were equally disillusioned. Half of their Confederacy's fighting men had died during the battles against New France while their erstwhile enemies in Canada seemed stronger than ever. Their chiefs realized they had been duped, and they vowed never again to take up sides in future conflicts.

In 1702 the Five Nations were wooed by the British and the French but they had learned their lesson. A few remained loyal to the British Crown but many others joined their late adversaries and became Christians at the Caughnawaga mission on the St. Lawrence and at other missions in Canada.

During Queen Anne's War the French wisely chose not to provoke the Iroquois and confined their warlike activities to New England. In this war the English promised the colonists wholehearted support, calling for a large-scale raid into Canada by way of Lake Champlain.

King George's war began in 1744 but there was little involvement by the people of upstate New York and, in particular, the thoroughly disillusioned Iroquois. The French had built a new fortress at Louisbourg on Cape Breton Island that was considered impregnable. New England provincials captured it, much to the astonishment of Canadian commanders.

The war plodded on with only minor flare ups or massacres until it ended in 1748. The colonists had lived through another bloody, inconclusive war that had gained them nothing. But war between such long-term adversaries had not ended. It would take one more war between the British and the French to end the slaughter of their people on America's new frontiers.

The lakes of Champlain and St. Sacrement (Lake George) remained unsettled throughout the long years of warfare, despite their great beauty and possibilities for development. A vast, empty wilderness surrounded the lakes, with most of the Adirondacks devoid of permanent Indian inhabitants. The Adirondacks and the Catskills were hunting grounds for several tribes but the winters were too long to grow any of the crops that the Iroquois cultivated in the Mohawk Valley and throughout the center of the state.

Now that relative peace had returned to colonial America, its citizens strove to consolidate territories in which they lived in lieu of expanding into almost uncharted wilderness. During this period there were no permanent English settlements north of Albany. The few settlers who had claimed land, particularly around Wood Creek, departed once the militia were removed.

The French thought differently. Through the years they had made several attempts to occupy the Lake Champlain area. First, stockades or small forts were erected. The first extensive fortification was made in 1730 on a low headland that thrust out toward a bluff on the west shore. The French named the site "Pointe a la Chevelure" or "Hair of the Head Point." In colloquial language it became "Scalp Point," which the English mistranslated to "Crown Point," the name by which it is known today. The fort was near the site of the earlier stockade, an ideal location because the lake narrows here so that a musket ball would carry almost shore-to-shore. It was strengthened later when it became Fort St. Frédéric in 1749. It was believed the fort's guns would prevent entry by an invader into the lower part of the lake. Thus fortified, the French claimed the whole region as part of New France in the face of repeated protests from New York's colonial legislators. Settlers refused to move to this "empty wilderness" despite inducements by the French government and the protection offered by the forts.

The French proved more successful in their drive to explore and colonize the west.

After Major General Edward Braddock arrived in America in January of 1755, he met with colonial governors in Alexandria, Virginia, and proposed a triple strike against the French. He said that he and his regulars and provincial troops would sweep westward against Fort Duquesne in Ohio country. A colonial force under Governor William Shirley of Massachusetts would attack French forts at Niagara, while a third army of colonial troops would assemble at Albany, go up the Hudson River, cross over to Lake George and then attack Fort St. Frédéric at Crown Point.

Braddock's army suffered a disastrous ambush and had to retreat. After a series of vicious battles in upstate New York, and the fall of Quebec to the British and Americans, the Treaty of Paris awarded New France to the British on September 8, 1759, and it went out of existence.

Veterans of the long series of wars received warrants for land in lieu of pensions. A field officer was entitled to 5,000 acres, and other ranks received varying amounts, with corporals getting 200 acres and privates 100. Most of them sold out to speculators for cash. British Major Philip Skene decided to use his warrant to develop a baronial-type residence on Lake Champlain. Businessman William Gililland did the same, but increased his acreage by buying up warrants. Skene created his settlement, which included a large Parliamentary grant, at the head of Lake Champlain, where Wood Creek empties into South Bay. He placed 30 settlers, and later some slaves, on the grant even before it was officially approved by the Lords of Trade, while he continued his military career. They finally approved his claim and he added even more tracts to bring his total to 29,000 acres. The estate was called Skenesborough, and it was located on the present-day site of Whitehall. Although nothing remains of Skenesborough, he built a community unlike any other on the lake, where his settlers raised crops, cattle and horses. Later he acquired 600 acres rich in iron ore, which eventually became Port Henry. Although he was constantly in need of money due to his expansion of Skenesborough, he established a prosperous colony for the settlers.

In 1775, when most Americans favored independence from Great Britain, Skenes remained loyal. His son and daughters were made prisoners and his possessions were seized. He was jailed as a British official. After the war he was granted partial compensation by the British government for his losses, but the Americans refused to restore his property. Skenesborough was forfeited to New York State and its name was changed to Whitehall in 1788.

Private William Gililland had served for four years with the 35th Regiment of Foot and was discharged in 1758. A native of Ireland, he chose to remain in the colonies and established a merchandise business in New York. He married his partner's daughter Elizabeth. He had been given a warrant for 100 acres in the Champlain area and, after a visit to the region, he fell in love with it. Like Skenes he dreamed of acquiring large land holdings. After buying warrants, he led 13 men and three women plus cattle to the head of Lake George in 1765. By now he owned several thousand acres at the mouth of the Boquet River, and called his settlement Milltown (later known as Willsboro.) There he built a communal log house and erected a sawmill on the falls of the Boquet River.

He also laid out sites for future towns in the region. One, at the mouth of the Salmon River, he named Janesboro in honor of one of his daughters. Bessport was established in what is now Westport in honor of another of his daughters. He started another settlement on Cumberland Head near Plattsburgh which he named Charlottesboro for still another daughter. Elizabeth, on the site of present-day Essex, was named for his wife.

Gilliland brought his family to the area in 1766 and established a more democratic rule than was generally permissible in those colonial times. He allowed his settlers to hold a town meeting on March 17, 1767, where they signed an instrument for local government. Skenes considered such action heresy but Gilliland countered with the claim that they needed their own system of government because New York State law had not been extended to the wilderness with agents to maintain it.

When the American Revolution began in 1775 most settlers fled the Lake Champlain-Lake George region, but Gilliland refused to leave. He sold cattle and farm produce to the various American military groups that came through the area. The quartermaster of these outfits promised to pay but rarely was Gilliland ever compensated for his patriotism.

Unlike Skenes, Gilliland was an outspoken critic of British rule in the colonies, demanding more rights for the colonies. He and Moses Pierson, founder of Shelburne on the lake's eastern side, organized a company of Minutemen in 1777. They proposed a plan for seizing Ticonderoga, Crown Point and the king's armed vessel to win the entire command of Lake George and Lake Champlain. General Guy Carleton, Canada's governor, promptly offered a reward of 100 pounds for Gililland's capture.

The efforts by Skene and Gililland to settle the Champlain Valley were noteworthy examples of men who tried to bring civilization to this wilderness area. Few others were as successful. At the first sign of renewed war, they hastily left the region and most never returned.

Ethan Allen, and his irreverent Green Mountain Boys, decided to take the undermanned Fort Ticonderoga from its British garrison in 1775. Colonel Benedict Arnold had been empowered by the State of Massachusetts on May 3 to raise an army for the same purpose and he tried to assume command of Allen's men. But he arrived in Vermont with no soldiers. Allen's men loudly proclaimed they would serve no other man but Ethan and that ended the matter. Due to a lack of boats only 85 men of Allen's force set out for Fort Ticonderoga with Arnold tagging along. Finding the sentries all asleep, they easily penetrated the fort's defenses and captured it without firing a shot.

In another operation, Skenesborough was captured and Major Skene's son, Andrew Philip Skene, was made a prisoner. Fifty tenants and 12 slaves, plus a new schooner named *Liberty*, were taken into custody. Two days later the fort at the head of Lake George was captured by a small contingent from Fort Edward.

The capture of the forts was significant but their armament was even more valuable to the American cause. At Ticonderoga and Crown Point 120 cannon, six of them 24-pounders, became valuable spoils of war along with carloads of smaller guns, ammunition and food.

The British developed a familiar plan to defeat the Continental Army by sending a fleet of ships to sweep Lake Champlain of

American warships, and then send an army to take the now decrepit forts. The plan called for the army to move south towards Albany and merge with Sir William Howe's army which, after taking New York, would move up the Hudson River with Vice-Admiral Richard Howe's ships to Albany. It was believed that such a joint action would sever the New England states from the rest of the American colonies.

At this critical juncture in the fate of the newly-established nation, one of the most inept of the northern region's commanders was placed in charge of defending the Champlain Valley. Brigadier General Horatio Gates's main talent was in furthering his own career. He was militarily inept, but the army he took over from Brigadier John Sullivan after the ill-fated attack on Quebec was in a state that would have defied the abilities of a military genius.

The inhabitants of the Champlain region, particularly those in Vermont, appealed to Gates for protection, but he had no men to spare from Ticonderoga. Panic dominated the thoughts of the early settlers at each new rumor that Sir Guy Carleton's fleet and the British army were on their way. But the British general was in no hurry. The situation was further complicated by the animosity of the people who had settled in what were to become the states of Vermont and New Hampshire against New Yorkers in general and the Continental Congress in particular. Most of these people, but not all, rejoiced at the Declaration of Independence approved by the Congress on July 4, 1776.

While Gates frantically sought reinforcements, the gravity of the situation brought men in increasing numbers to defend the Champlain area, although supplies were not as easily forthcoming. Many of the new men succumbed to the lingering diseases spread by the veterans of the Canadian invasion.

Meanwhile, General Washington's troops were driven from Long Island, while Carleton still dallied in Montreal. His delay gave Gates precious time to rebuild Ticonderoga and prepare it for the inevitable attack. Crown Point was all but abandoned, although the east shore was stripped of its trees and a star-shaped fort emerged, along with a hospital and barracks. With guns mounted there, and Ticonderoga easily strengthened, it was believed that the narrow lake at this point could be more easily defended and offer protection against enemy forces entering the upper part of Lake Champlain. This area wound through swamps for 15 miles to Skenesborough and South Bay.

Despite Gates's conviction that Ticonderoga was impregnable, he and his engineers over-looked a basic defect in their defense plans. Sugar Loaf Mountain (the British later called it Mount Defiance), south and west of Fort Ticon-deroga, was 572 feet higher than Mount Independence. It was little more than a mile from it and the fort on the op-posite side. It was half encir-cled by Lake George's outlet. If guns were placed upon its crest, they would dominate the entire area. This was pointed

Benedict Arnold. Appointed a colonel, he was later promoted to major general.

out by Benedict Arnold to Gates and Schuyler but they insisted it would be impossible to place guns on the crest of Sugar Loaf Mountain. They had the arguments of previous commanders to back them up, but they were all tragically wrong.

In mid-summer of 1776 Gates wrote to General Washington, "As soon as all the vessels and gondolas are equipped, General Arnold has offered to go to Crown Point and take command of them. This is exceedingly pleasing to me, as he has a perfect knowledge of maritime affairs and is, besides, a most deserving and gallant officer." He later regretted his laudatory words.

Although the American fleet was still unfinished Benedict Arnold, who had been promoted to brigadier general after the Canadian invasion, took command of the old *Enterprise* that he had seized at St. Johns. He also had Major Skene's former trading schooner *Liberty,* and the *Royal Savage* that had just been completed at Ticonderoga. These were light ships, compared to the British fleet, and equipped with three- and four-pound cannon. Arnold also took over command of 10 gunboats. Only 70 of the men who manned his fleet had previous ship experience and the remainder of the crewmen were army soldiers who had been drafted for his command.

Arnold led his small fleet downlake at the first sign that Carleton was prepared to move against Ticonderoga. He had no illusions about defeating the British fleet but he wanted to place his ships in a position where they could take their greatest toll of the enemy.

With this strategy uppermost in his mind, he moved his small fleet to a position between Valcour Island and the western shore on September 23. There the water was deep, with a narrow passage. He believed Carleton would have difficulty reaching him here and then only with a few ships at a time. Arnold's fleet was again reinforced with the galleys *Trumbull, Washington* and *Congress.* Arnold shifted his command from the schooner *Royal Savage* to the *Congress.* A guard boat fired a warning October 11 that Carleton's fleet was in sight and scuttled back to the protection of Arnold's fleet.

The schooner *Maria* led Carleton's fleet, commanded by Captain Thomas Pringle. The British fleet moved south beyond Valcour, although Arnold's presence must have been known to him. Then Pringle ordered his ships to claw back into the north wind to make contact with Arnold's fleet.

For Arnold the situation was impossible, although Pringle's error in seamanship gave him precious time to array his ships for battle. The British had 700 experienced soldiers and sailors while Arnold's 500 men had varying degrees of competence. Pringle's clumsy handling of the situation was viewed with contempt by his officers as he tried to tack into the wind and come around the southern tip of Valcour. His gunboats made it because they were rowed and they came into range before Pringle's heavier ships. Indians whooped and yelled on the island, firing their muskets at Arnold's fleet, but the distance was too great for effective firing.

The British warships were armed with heavy bow cannon and a score of soldiers and sailors. They spread out across the south entrance to Arnold's position. Now the *Carleton* rushed through the line of gunboats and dropped anchor in front of the American fleet positioned in a crescent facing to the south. The *Royal Savage* and the gondolas immediately attacked the *Carleton* and damaged her so severely that she had to be towed out of the battle. Now it was the *Royal Savage*'s turn to bear the brunt of iron balls, as the *Inflexible* caught her while she attempted to turn upwind. Due to her inexperienced crew, the *Royal Savage* got hung up and the British ship fired a broadside into her at close range. Her crew ran her ashore on the south tip of Valcour and began to desert her. A British crew under Lieutenant Edward Longcraft's command from the *Loyal Convert* gondola boarded the *Royal Savage* and captured some of her crew while the remainder fled to the island. The *Royal Savage*'s guns were now turned on other ships in Arnold's fleet. While Longcraft frantically signaled to Pringle to draw off his prize, the fleet's commander seemed in a daze, unable to understand what was going on about him. Longcraft, with half of his men either killed or wounded, finally had to abandon the *Royal Savage*. Indians plundered the ship and she was burned to the water line.

The battle between Arnold's fleet and the British gunboats intensified, while Pringle's more powerful ships remained outside the fray. The battle continued all afternoon, becoming so intense that the wooded island was set on fire. The British gunboats, comprised of only one-third of the fleet, withdrew at 5 o'clock because they were out of ammunition.

Arnold's inexperienced crew had performed magnificently, but he noticed that the gondola *Philadelphia* was sinking, while two others were under water. The galley *Washington* was barely able to stay afloat and Arnold's flagship *Congress* was full of holes and in a precarious condition. Sixty men had been killed or wounded, and only a fourth of the fleet's ammunition was left. The British lost only two gunboats while a third blew up. Arnold's inexperienced gunners failed to make consistent hits although the gunboats were stationary targets. Carleton claimed the loss of eight killed and six wounded, but such a low figure defies credibility.

Arnold held a meeting with his captains to assess the situation. All agreed it was desperate. The decision was made to withdraw his battered fleet. Incredibly, Pringle failed to guard the entrances, permitting Arnold's ships to draw off to the south.

Carleton and Pringle awoke the next morning to resume the battle but lo and behold Arnold's ships were gone. Still they dallied for another 24 hours before taking off in pursuit. Arnold's fleet could easily have been destroyed if the British commander had followed them. The Americans were only eight miles away, shielded by Schuyler Island, as Arnold urged his men to repair the battered ships for travel up the lake. Most of Arnold's men escaped, but the majority of his ships were abandoned and burned.

With another harsh winter approaching, Carleton ordered his campaign ended in mid-November and his ships and army returned to Canada. This news was greeted with relief by Gates and the 9,000 Continental troops and militia stationed at Ticonderoga.

The northern campaign of 1776 had achieved a modest success. It gave the Americans time to strengthen their armed forces and to impose capitulation of the British army at Saratoga the following year. But Arnold's success in delaying the invasion for a year through the efforts of his small fleet was largely due to Pringle's incredible lack of professional ability. His own officers called him a coward. Then, too, Carleton's unshakeable belief that kindness would end the war with the rebels must be taken into account. At the very least, Pringle could have been more aggressive. His highest ranking subordinates said "he could hardly have done less."

Although the winter months precluded any further British invasion through the Champlain Valley, General Washington's Continental Army at Trenton, New Jersey was beset by a much larger British army and faced destruction. Gates stripped the fort at Ticonderoga of all militia regiments and went with them to join General Washington's army. The men remained there while he hastened to Baltimore where a fearful Congress had retreated. There Gates pleaded to be given Major General Philip Schuyler's job as commander of the Northern Department, despite his disgraceful record in the field.

Washington's army defeated the Hessians at Trenton, and then the British at Princeton, as fighting largely ceased for the winter. Washington's Continental Army spent the winter at Morristown while Howe's British army largely evacuated the state of New Jersey.

While Major General John Burgoyne at the Canadian end of the lake prepared his 7,200 professional soldiers, 250 Canadians and Tories, and 400 Indians to move against the Americans, Brigadier General Arthur St. Clair, who had succeeded Gates as battlefield commander, strengthened Fort Ticonderoga's defenses. He reduced the size of Gate's widespread defense network so it could be easily defended by his 2,800-man garrison.

Burgoyne's army moved south in June, 1777. Although its leader was incompetent, the rest of the top officers were professionals with well-trained British soldiers and Hessian mercenaries.

Other than Fort Ticonderoga, the New York frontier was almost defenseless. St. Clair waited until the invasion was underway before he summoned additional militia. Such a decision was forced upon him by the shortage of provisions at Ticonderoga.

The bands played and there was an air of optimism as Burgoyne's army embarked on ships at St. Johns. Like every commander

British Major General John Burgoyne, in a painting by Sir Joshua Reynolds. (The Frick Collection, New York)

before him, Burgoyne soon regretted his decision to include Indian warriors. He told his officers "that a Thousand Savages brought into the field cost more then 20,000 men." He was particularly concerned by reports of earlier field commanders that the Indians easily got out of control and reverted to revolting attacks against white prisoners. In a speech to Indian leaders Burgoyne said their warriors could continue the practice of taking scalps of dead men but he warned, "On no account or pretense or subtlety or prevarication are they to be taken from the wounded or even dying and still less pardonable if possible will it be held to kill men in this condition."

Indian leaders promised faithfully they would abide by his instruction. He should have known better after the atrocities that had been inflicted by the Indians on both sides against soldiers and innocent civilians alike.

After his troops occupied Crown Point on June 27, 1777, Burgoyne issued a proclamation to residents of the area. He said he would welcome Tories, give protection to all those who remained neutral and that his army would pay for all provisions.

Burgoyne was now ready to move against Ticonderoga, personally well-equipped to withstand the rigors of battle, with a mistress and a well-stocked wagon train of wine.

St. Clair hastily ordered additional militia from northern regional commander Major General Philip Schuyler and 900 men were dispatched. Two of the Massachusetts regiments took this opportunity to announce that their time of service was about to expire and that they were going home. Fortunately Burgoyne's early attack prevented their departure.

The British moved against the fort by land and water. British troops marched along Champlain's west shore while the Germans moved along the east. On July 2 the American guns on Mount Independence, manned by soldier-of-fortune Roche de Fermoy, opened fire against the Hessian troops and stopped their advance.

This action kept the road clear to the east. But the British continued to move along the west shore. Heavy guns were placed on Mount Hope, overlooking the Lake George outlet, and St. Clair's artillery could not dislodge them. Meanwhile, St. Clair ordered his troops to withdraw from this section, destroying the blockhouses before they separated.

The next day British and German troops split their forces and moved to the left and right to cut off the Ticonderoga peninsula from the mainland.

General William Phillips, in charge of artillery for the British command, and the officer responsible for taking Mount Hope, met with Burgoyne and discussed Sugar Loaf Mountain. No other British commander appreciated the fact that this mountain was the key to Fort Ticonderoga. It was always considered impossible to haul cannon up its slopes to the top where they could fire inside the fort and make it untenable. Phillips was convinced it was scalable and he proved it could be done by ordering his men to haul cannon to its top. Even General Schuyler, who had often demonstrated his outstanding qualities as a military commander had failed to realize that heavy guns on that mountain would make the fort indefensible. After guns were placed on top, the British changed the mountain's name to Mount Defiance.

After the first 12-pounders were installed on the peak, St. Clair knew that he had no chance of holding the fort. He decided to abandon it that night while the American guns on Mount Independence kept the road open to the east. He ordered noncombatants, women and the sick, to be evacuated by bateaux, escorted by 500 troops and five galleys. A schooner, the last remnant of the Champlain fleet, was sunk to keep it out of British hands.

Burgoyne's officers were unaware of the garrison's departure until Roche de Fermoy, before leaving Mount Independence, set fire to his quarters and the flames revealed their departure to the British. Hessian and British troops took off after the retreating column. A series of misfortunes dogged St. Clair's troops. He had ordered the

Major General Philip Schuyler, an aristocrat, was chosen to command the patriots in the northern theater of war. (Library of Congress)

main fort to be blown up but the men delegated to light the powder failed to do so. He had also ordered cannon placed at the east end of the bridge to fire at British troops as they advanced. The four men detailed for this job found a keg of Madeira wine and the British captured them dead drunk. Unfortunately for American commanders, abject drunkenness was common throughout the war and frequently interfered with the orderly discipline so necessary on a battlefield. British troops were more disciplined and alcohol was not so readily available to the common soldier.

Most of St. Clair's men fared better and they were kept well ahead of the advancing British. They arrived safely at Castleton, Vermont.

Gates had established a chain boom to prevent British ships from entering this channel but British sappers cut it in half an hour. Now ships entered the channel and took off after the fleeing Americans. They had reached Skenesborough by 3 p.m., happy that they had come through unscathed. Two hours later British gunboats closed in on the galleys protecting the non-combatants and captured two of them while driving three others ashore. British troops now landed at the town and attacked its stockade. The defenders had to flee southward for the relative safety of Fort Ann.

Burgoyne garrisoned Ticonderoga and hastened the majority of his army to Skenesborough. Some of St. Clair's men disobeyed orders to press on to Castleton and spent the night at a lesser distance. British troops surprised them on July 7, killing and wounding a number of them while the rest fled. St. Clair's main army joined General Schuyler near Fort Edward five days later without further incident because Burgoyne abandoned further pursuit.

Burgoyne slowly advanced to the Hudson River by way of Skenesborough and Wood Creek, despite the fact that Lake George was the way of least resistance. Burgoyne explained his reasoning by saying that if his army had been ordered to return to Ticonderoga to start another route through Lake George the morale of this men would have suffered.

The British reached the abandoned base at Fort Edward on July 30 and Schuyler ordered a withdrawal to Stillwater. He had no choice and it was a sound move, but it disturbed the Congress and the people in the region.

Burgoyne had accomplished more than any French or British commander had ever done, and he was confident the rebel territory would be split. With his troops on the upper reaches of the Hudson River, and the territory between him and Canada all secured, Burgoyne was ready to make his final move on the direct water route to Albany.

In western New York Colonel St. Leger brought his British forces to Fort Stanwix (now Fort Schuyler) near Rome on August 12. Schuyler sent Benedict Arnold with a small force to relieve the fort. Arnold tried a bluff, and it worked. He announced that he was moving

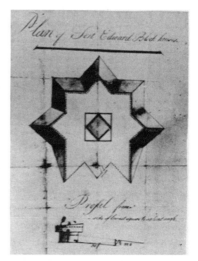

Fort Edward. This drawing shows the original plan for the blockhouse. (Metropolitan Museum of Art, New York)

against St. Leger with a vast army. The news panicked the Indians with St. Leger and they quickly departed for Canada. Then the Loyalists left him. St. Leger hastily withdrew to Oswego.

Meanwhile the Howe brothers' advance up the Hudson from New York hadn't even started. Furthermore, they had no intention of participating. They believed that after the fall of Ticonderoga Burgoyne didn't need their support.

Although the Howe brothers had been ordered by their superiors in London to advance up the Hudson and join Burgoyne's army, the orders were mislaid and never sent. Burgoyne received the disturbing news from General Howe on August 3 that his army was moving toward Philadelphia instead of following the original plans. Burgoyne's army at Fort Edward was now in dire straits, although he didn't realize it at first. He gave orders to advance. He

Sir William Howe. From a 1777 English print, Howe is shown with the Order of the Bath, awarded by the King for his victory over the Americans in the Battle of Long Island. (United States Naval Institute)

was shocked to learn on August 17 that only 400 men returned of the 1,000 he had sent against the American supply depot at Bennington, Vermont. And, on August 22, he was informed that St. Leger had abandoned the siege of Stanwix and begun his retreat to Canada. Burgoyne's Indian allies, sensing a familiar debacle, began to desert and only a few remained. His proud army was down to 4,000 men, but he ordered it to press on against the Americans. On September 13, it crossed to the west bank of the Hudson.

By now Brigadier General Benjamin Lincoln had rounded up 2,500 local and Massachusetts militia at Pawlet. He sent 1,500 of these men to Lake Champlain to attack British supply lines by seizing Skenesborough and Ticonderoga. In 1775 Colonel John Brown had proposed a similar raid. At that time, Ethan Allen led 500 soldiers against Fort Ticonderoga. This time Colonel Johnson of Massachusetts was assigned another 500 men to attack Mount Independence while the remaining third under Colonel Woodbridge were sent to capture Skenesborough.

On the day that Burgoyne's army crossed to the west side of the Hudson River, the expedition set out. Four days later Brown's men captured Skenesborough without a fight. Fearful of a sharp British reaction to this raid, Lincoln moved his other 1,000 men to Skenesborough to reinforce Brown's expedition.

Brigadier General Henry Watson, who commanded the garrison at Ticonderoga, held the rebels in such disdain that he took few precautions against a raid on the fort. He was busy forwarding supplies to Burgoyne's army in the south via the direct route up Lake George. The British didn't react to the attack on Skenesborough because they didn't learn of it until late on September 17. By then the blockhouse on Mount Defiance had been seized by Captain Ebenezer Allen with 60 men. A six-pound cannon had been used to signal sunrise and sunset and when it was used to fire on Allen's men, General Powell realized something was wrong. After capturing Mount Defiance, Brown's men attacked the Lake George landing where 50 bateaux, 17 gunboats and a sloop were anchored. They were all seized, the protecting blockhouse was destroyed, and their defenders captured.

Brown now led his men down the outlet. At the sawmill they ran into a large British force still sound asleep. They hadn't heard the firing because of the roar of the falls. Here 150 more bateaux and two brass cannon were captured.

Brown's men now crossed the outlet bridge and moved up the hill toward the old French defense line. Another detail of British soldiers was found guarding 100 prisoners, who were soon set free and joined forces with the enterprising Brown.

It was at this juncture that the signal gun on Mount Defiance began to boom and General Powell ordered his men to fall back into the fort while he assessed the situation. Ships on the lake and shore batteries began to fire at random, without shooting at any specific targets. Now that the fort was prepared to contest any attempt at entry, Brown's and Johnson's men abandoned any attempt to attack it. The British and the Americans had an equal number of men but the British were behind stout fortifications that were impregnable unless heavy siege guns were available. They were not, so the Americans acted wisely.

Brown tried to bluff his way in. He sent General Powell a letter that the fort was surrounded by "the Mighty Army of the Continent" and should surrender. Powell replied, "The Garrison entrusted to my charge I shall defend to the last."

After the Americans ran out of ammunition they withdrew. Brown could have captured Ticonderoga if he had been assisted by the 1,000 men whom Lincoln had hurried back to Vermont without a fight, and if he had been adequately equipped with cannon. Although the capture of Fort Ticonderoga would have forced Burgoyne to surrender for lack of supplies, his fate was sealed during a series of battles in and around Saratoga.

Arnold returned to headquarters after St. Leger's army gave up the battle to occupy the Mohawk Valley, only to find that his old nemesis Major General Horatio Gates had finally succeeded in ousting Schuyler as commander of the Northern Department.

On September 19 the British Army moved against the American camp at Saratoga in three separate columns. Two forced their way through heavy forests while the third column of German troops marched along the Hudson River. American scouts reported the British advance to Gates who ordered Colonel Daniel Morgan's Virginia riflemen to report their progress. Morgan's men encountered the advance guard of the British center force about 12:30 p.m. and a brief skirmish occurred at Freeman's farm, a mile north of the American camp.

Regis Heights, near Stillwater, had been fortified because it was considered the best defensive position to stop Burgoyne's march towards Albany. Arnold commanded the left wing. Although Gates was opposed, Arnold ordered his troops to attack. His action brought on a general escalation of the battle, forcing Gates' hand.

For the next three hours the two armies fought inconclusively, although the British were forced to retreat before the superior forces arrayed against them whose deadly fire took a heavy toll. The battle reversed itself when the German mercenaries, who had followed the Hudson River, moved against the American right flank. Burgoyne now succeeded in taking the initiative and the American troops were forced to retreat. A shortage of ammunition among the American ranks proved crucial. Otherwise they might have defeated Burgoyne's army the first day. Gates, in his report to

Congress, pointedly refrained from mentioning Arnold's decisive action and removed him from command of the left wing.

Although both sides claimed victory, the British and the Hessians lost twice as many as the Americans. The two armies were now a mile apart. The heavy casualties Burgoyne's army had suffered played an important role in events yet to come. The British commander ordered his army to entrench in the vicinity of the Freeman farm while he pleaded for Howe's support to relieve his precarious position by moving north, instead of to Philadelphia. Burgoyne waited for three weeks with his entrenched army until he realized that Howe had no intention of aiding him. His situation was critical because the American army had been growing steadily larger while his supply lines to Canada remained in a precarious condition. He was faced with two hard choices – retreating to Canada or pushing on to Albany without support from the Howe brothers. He chose to fight a second engagement. On October 7 he ordered a reconnaissance-in-force to test the American left flank. It was ably led and was supported by eight cannon and a force of 1,500 men. After marching in a southwesterly direction the troops were deployed in a clearing on the Barber farm. The British faced an open field but both flanks rested in woods. This latter condition exposed them to a surprise attack.

The Americans attacked at about 3 p.m. in three columns under Colonel Morgan, Brigadier General Ebenezer Learned and Brigadier General Enoch Poor. They repeatedly broke through the British lines, but the enemy troops rallied and fought back until both flanks had to give ground under the fierce American attacks. General Simon Fraser, in command of the British right, was mortally wounded when he rode among his men to encourage them to make a stand and cover the army's withdrawal.

Benedict Arnold, who had been relieved of command after a quarrel with Gates, now rode out to lead Learned's brigade against the Hessian troops holding the British center. These troops were part of the general withdrawal, retreating to make a stand in the fortifications on Freeman's farm. With the battle only an hour old,

*Surrender at Saratoga. In John Trumbull's painting of the ceremony,
Burgoyne offers his sword to Gates, as Daniel Morgan, in white
deerskin, and other officers attend America's first triumph of the
Revolution. Philip Schuyler is third from left.*
(New York Public Library)

Burgoyne had lost eight cannon and more than 40 officers and
men.

Sensing victory, Arnold led a column in a series of attacks on the
Balcarres Redoubt, a strong British fortified position on the Freeman farm. Despite valiant attempts to overwhelm the redoubt, the
British troops held fast. Arnold wheeled his horse and, dashing
through crossfire of both armies, spurred northwest to the Balcarres Redoubt. He arrived just as American troops began their as-
sault on the fortification. He joined in the final attempt and helped
to overwhelm the German soldiers defending it. Upon entering the
redoubt his horse was killed and Arnold was wounded in the same
leg that had been wounded at Quebec. A Gate's aide hurried to the
front with a message that Arnold must leave immediately for the
rear.

Burgoyne now began a slow retreat but the Americans had put entrenchments at all the fords and effectively closed the Hudson crossings. Nightfall ended the fighting with Burgoyne's troops occupying a fortified camp on the heights of Saratoga. The American army, swelled to more than 20,000 men, surrounded Burgoyne's 6,000 troops. He had no choice but to seek terms and he surrendered on October 17. His army marched out "with the honors of war" and stacked their weapons on the west bank of the Hudson River.

Arnold's brave action in rallying the men and forcing Burgoyne's army to retreat was widely praised. Congress restored his precedence in rank as a major general. He was carried to Albany and honored as a hero.

At Ticonderoga, when General Powell received word about Burgoyne's surrender, he recalled his troops from Lake George, burned the installations on Mount Defiance and tried to blow up Fort Ticonderoga, but he wasn't successful. Powell had earlier lost all his boats, so his garrison struck out on foot for Canada. They didn't get away unscathed. Captain Ebenezer Allen and 50 Rangers followed closely behind them. Near the mouth of the Boquet River on November 12 they caught up with the British general's rear guard. They captured horses, cattle and other valuables along with 59 men and Dinah Mattis, a negro slave and her child, whom Allen set free.

The major battles now shifted away from Lake Champlain and Lake George, although British ships continued to control Lake Champlain. From time to time their ships brought raiding parties into Vermont and the New York shore. But the ground fighting had shifted to Georgia and Virginia and the lake region was stripped of men who were needed to fight battles in the south with Washington's army. One British detachment raided as far as Saratoga but it didn't have the strength to control the area. Canadian Indians occasionally swarmed through settlements in upstate New York and in Vermont causing terror and suffering to those who vowed not to be driven from their homes. The people of Vermont, who adopted their own Constitution in 1777, now considered themselves a separate republic. Therefore the British tried to divide the region's people from the rest of the United States, first with raids and then with subversion. Although Vermonters felt alone and unappreciated they remained steadfast in maintaining their independence. Vermont became the 14th State in 1791.

Benedict Arnold joined General Washington's army at Valley Forge in Pennsylvania in 1778. When the British evacuated Philadelphia, he was assigned as the city's military commander.

Some of his reputation as a national hero began to erode when his lavish life style and his friendship with Loyalists in the city became known. When he married Margaret "Peggy" Shippen, 18-year-old daughter of a Loyalist in 1779, his reputation was further tarnished. It went into serious decline after he was accused of misusing public property and authority. In the face of these charges he resigned his command. When General Washington delayed action on his court martial Arnold secretly offered his services to the British. They were accepted with enthusiasm and promises of reward were made by Major John André, aide to Sir Henry Clinton, British commander-in-chief. Arnold now routinely supplied the British with military intelligence.

Meanwhile, he faced a court martial in December and was convicted the following month in 1780 of using army wagons to haul his personal goods. Congress approved the verdict and he was issued a reprimand.

Now fully committed to helping the British cause he sought command of West Point, New York, from his friend General Schuyler and his request was granted. He also began converting his assets into cash so they could be shifted to London.

Arnold wrote to André on July 15, 1780, and offered to surrender the garrison at West Point for 20,000 English pounds. Clinton agreed. Then André was picked up in disguise by American soldiers with papers incriminating him and Arnold. When Arnold learned of André's capture, he knew his treason would be exposed. He escaped down the Hudson to New York City where his wife was later permitted to join him.

He fought against Americans in Virginia and this former American hero became a pariah in the United States, while his life in Great Britain following the war was that of a social outcast.

Arnold's motive for changing sides evidently was purely personal. He had lust for money, his vanity was outraged by the shoddy treatment he had sometimes received, and he had sworn vengeance against the Congress for wrongs they purportedly had done to him.

General Washington's defeat of the British Army under Lord Cornwallis on October 19, 1781 effectively ended the war in the upstate New York area after one-third of all battles had been fought in the state. Great Britain, eager for peace in America because of conflicts with European nations, in 1782 recognized American independence in the Peace of Paris signed the following year. It gave the new republic 29 years of peace.

Settlers slowly began to return to the Champlain Valley after the war, with the Vermont side gaining the lion's share because of the more arable land for miles inland compared to the New York shore. There the Adirondacks intruded, making farming a risky enterprise. But slowly the western side of Lake Champlain began to be populated. Usually rivers attracted people to a site. Prime requisites for any kind of settlement were a sawmill and a grist mill, and these had to be water-powered. Plattsburgh began to grow when such mills used the waters of the Saranac River in 1785, although growth was slow. In 1811 the town had only 78 dwellings but the Plattsburgh Academy was built this year. It was the largest structure in northern New York and fed the desires of the populace for higher education for their children. Trade with Canada, and the opening up of the Adirondacks to lumbering and mining, helped to make it the largest city in the Adirondack region. At first potash, created from wood ash, was the principal money-making product.

Settlers who prospered in the Adirondack region were those who were self-sufficient, using hard currency only to purchase luxuries obtainable outside the region. Good neighbors willingly lent a hand to raise a barn or join in threshing or taking part in a husking bee. The host was expected to supply the liquor, and God help the man who ran out before the job was done!

Americans resented the continual presence of British army posts on American soil. The British maintained a garrison at Point au Fer in the early 1790s, and at Blockhouse Point. A British ship, the *Maria*, maintained a station in the channel between Point au Fer and Alburg to inspect all north-bound American boats. American ships were compelled to salute the British ensign and, if they didn't, they were fired upon. The Jay Treaty of 1796 finally eliminated the presence of this small British force.

The Champlain Valley underwent one final climactic battle during the War of 1812. Commodore Thomas Macdonough won a great victory over a British fleet at Plattsburgh by capturing a frigate, a brig and two sloops. The results of the battle on September 11, 1814, had world-wide implications because it was as decisive a naval battle as any ever fought. This victory more than any other action brought British negotiators inclined to end the conflict to the bargaining table. Otherwise the war might have been prolonged with ever-increasing casualties and with little political gain for either side.

Two weeks after a peace treaty between the United States and Great Britain was signed, a fact unknown to the participants, thousands of Wellington's veterans assaulted General Andrew Jackson's American defenses at New Orleans, but they were soundly defeated.

It had been a tragic war that should never have been fought. If there had been more understanding between officials of both countries, it might never have occurred. The war did serve to bring the people of the United States more closely together as one nation and not as a collection of separate states. After 200 years of conflict during the early years of their existence, an enduring peace has prevailed between the United States and its northern neighbor Canada since 1815.

One of the worst summers of harsh weather followed a warm, wet spring in the Adirondack region after the war ended. Snow fell in June and cold weather destroyed young crops. A hard freeze followed that proved devastating to the region's shorn sheep and they perished by the thousands. There were more snow flurries in July and August, but the rains did not come on schedule and late crops that had survived the earlier cold spell now succumbed to a freeze.

Settlers flocked to the Adirondack region following the end of the war, but the elements drove many of them to move to Ohio, believing such weather was typical. It is not, but they had no way of knowing that.

Cheese and butter became the area's principal cash products, particularly on farms near the Champlain shore. Now lumbering interests moved in and by the mid-1800s much of the Adirondack region was deforested of its old-growth timber. Unfortunately, most of the land laid bare was unfit for agriculture because of its hilly terrain.

Less than a year after Robert Fulton's steamboat *Clermont* made nautical history by traveling from New York to Albany on the Hudson River in 32 hours, the first steamboat was launched on Lake Champlain in 1808. The *Vermont* had a tall stack with a barge-like hull and open paddlewheels. After her launching, she was ridiculed when sailing vessels ran circles around her. But she was the first of a long line of steamers that transformed commerce on Lake Champlain and Lake George for the next 100 years. The *Vermont* sank in 1815 while traveling on the Richelieu River after breaking her connecting rod, which stabbed through her side. The third *Vermont* was built in 1903 by the Champlain Transportation Company and became the largest of the celebrated steamers, displacing 1,195 tons and able to steam at 23 miles an hour. Three years later the company put the excursion steamer *Ticonderoga* in service. By now railroads were taking the place of lake travel, and later competition from the automobile made such travel less inviting. But I vividly recall my many trips on the *Vermont* up and down the lake from Plattsburgh to Ticonderoga (with a stop at Burlington) in the 1920s, as one of the true delights of my younger years. Ferries still ply the lake, but the end of the steamboating era for passengers has never been adequately replaced by railroads or automobiles.

For years there were plans to build railroads into the Adirondacks but the formidable obstacles posed by the mountainous terrain discouraged most promoters. The first railroad to be completed into the Adirondacks ran from Plattsburgh to Saranac Lake and the first train to traverse the route made the run on December 5, 1887. The Chateaugay Railroad had completed what others had tried and failed to do. The state of New York built a line from Lake Champlain to Dannemora State Prison in 1879. When mining operations at Lyon Mountain proved feasible, the Chateaugay Railroad bought this line from the state and extended its tracks to Lyon Mountain. Again the line was extended to Standish, to Loon Lake and eventually to Saranac Lake in 1887. The Delaware and Hudson bought the Chateaugay Railroad on January 1, 1905 and broad-gauged the tracks. Once track was laid between Saranac Lake and Lake Placid, service commenced between the two villages. It cost $1 for the 10-mile trip. This line was eventually sold to the New York Central, which later became Penn-Central.

Now that these railroad pioneers had proved the feasibility of laying track across the rugged terrain in the Adirondacks, many others started their own railroads, particularly lumber tycoon John Hurd. Hurd's line was confined at first to Franklin County and entered the park at Le Boeuf's about 10 miles south of Santa Clara. The last link, the 22-mile section to Tupper Lake, was finished in 1889. It was primarily a logging train. This hard-driving, flamboyant man finally overextended himself and died a pauper. The New York Central inherited his line.

During the depression years in the 1930s the New York Central tried to keep its new extensive Adirondack trackage profitable by organizing ski trains. They proved to be popular. Along with daily freight trains, the New York Central provided a needed service but it became more and more a burden upon the rest of the system. In 1950 the New York Central petitioned the Public Service Commission to remove its more uneconomical routes. From then on, service was cut back year after year until the last passenger train departed Saranac Lake on April 24, 1965.

Next, freight service also became uneconomical and the New York Central refused to take shipments of less than carload bulk. For a while one freight train ran once a week, but all rail service came to an end in 1972. New York Central and the Pennsylvania Railroad merged in the hope that the surviving Penn-Central could achieve profitability on freight service alone.

AMTRAK was formed as a semi-government agency to maintain essential railroad passenger service but it has none in the Adirondacks. It does provide passenger service from New York to Montreal, with a stop at Westport on Lake Champlain. Busses are available to take passengers into the Adirondacks. This is a limited service. AMTRAK can be called on their toll-free (800) 872-7245 number for precise schedules. As we went to press, AMTRAK's schedule calls for departure from New York City's Penn Station at 7:15 a.m., with arrival in Westport at 12:51, Monday through Saturday. On Sunday the train leaves New York at 10:25 a.m. and arrives in Westport at 3:59 p.m. From Montreal, the train leaves at 11:00 a.m. and arrives at Westport at 2:34 p.m., Monday through Saturday. On Sunday the train leaves the Canadian city at 12:40 p.m. and arrives in Westport at 4:12 p.m. AMTRAK has a special ski package. For details call (800) 899-2558.

The region's lumber business had become uneconomical by the mid-1850s. The cause was a familiar one – over-cutting. When iron ore was discovered in upstate New York, particularly in Essex and Clinton counties, the lake towns enjoyed an economic revival. Iron production reached its peak in these two counties in 1880 when their mines produced 23% of the iron mined in the United States. But the Mesabi Range in Minnesota during the 1890s produced lower-cost iron and a majority of the Adirondack mines could no longer compete. Most mines shut down. My mother's father worked in the mines at Palmer Hill near Ausable Forks for many years before they were closed.

After the 18th amendment was passed in 1919, barring the making and distribution of alcoholic beverages, the Adirondacks became a war zone, pitting bootleggers and law enforcement officers against one another in an endless and fruitless battle. The goal was to keep alcohol from Canada out of the United States. Abuse of alcohol had become a national disgrace but this new law proved unenforceable. It made drinking romantic, adventurous and socially correct. Many young people who normally would not have been interested in heavy drinking found it the "in" thing to do. Most people ignored the law, believing their constitutional rights had been violated. A Prohibition Bureau was set up under the Treasury Department and began an initial recruitment of 1,512 officers. Eventually the total reached 3,000. These men were given little training, and many of them succumbed to the huge profits they could make by simply looking the other way. Most citizens and bootleggers detested them. They were considered dishonest and an expensive nuisance. Local police were particularly incensed by their intrusion into their communities. This small force had to control the Mexican and Canadian borders plus 18,000 miles of Atlantic and Pacific seacoasts. During the first 10 years they arrested 572,000 suspects, although only two-thirds were convicted. They seized 1,600,000 distilleries and stills, destroyed a billion gallons of malt liquor, hard cider and mash and captured 45,000 cars and 1,300 boats. Two thousand hoodlums and rum-runners were killed and the Adirondack region saw its fair share of these killings as agents raced after liquor-laden cars throughout the back roads of the mountains. Shots in the night, and often in the daytime, indicated all too clearly that another chase of a suspected rum-runner was on. Forty-horsepower (very powerful for this period) Cadillacs, Marmons, Stutz Bearcats, Packards and sometimes a Lincoln or Locomobile were popular among these rum-running jockeys who lived hard and dangerous lives and spent every dollar they made on equally fast living. In northern New York the "wild-west" lived again until President Franklin D. Roosevelt arranged to have the prohibition amendment repealed in 1932. It had solved nothing and created an underworld bureaucracy that used its ill-gotten gains to dominate other elements of American society.

New York State has weathered several industrial downturns that affected the Adirondacks, starting with a major depression in the 1930s that was only alleviated by World War II. The post-war economic boom was short-lived and by the 1950s upstate factories, mills and small businesses began to move south and west. In the next two decades peripheral cities in the Hudson and Mohawk valleys lost as much as 25% of their population. This situation had a serious impact on tourism and on the economy of the mountain region because there were no longer nearby industrial sites where residents could find jobs. The region's hard-hit economy was further weakened by a steep fall-off in the tourist business. The area's road infrastructure was allowed to decline, with Route 9 from Albany to Montreal, for example, remaining a two-lane highway in a sad state of disrepair.

The Region Today

Tourism has always been the region's most lucrative business and eventually steps were taken to improve the accessibility of the Adirondacks. With the opening of the New York State Thruway from New York to Buffalo, and the Northway in 1967 from Albany to Canada, the automobile opened up the mountains to millions of travelers, not least the 35 million who live within a day's drive of the region. Its remotest woods, peaks and waters, among the most primitive in the eastern U.S., are now easily accessible by modern highways – though there are still 12 wilderness areas that can be reached only on foot or by canoe. Large numbers of tourists can be accommodated in nearby villages and resorts or at state campsites along major highways. Still, in the northwest quarter there's a tract of 50,000 acres that has never been logged and remains a true wilderness. Throughout the forests, thousands of brooks and rivers cascade down countless mountain slopes to form hundreds of lakes and ponds.

But there is more to the Adirondacks than tourism. Lumbering, once the region's major industry, is still conducted at a reduced level on private lands. Several magnetite iron ore deposits are mined in the region. The Benson Mine near Star Lake is one of the largest such open-pit mines. The MacIntyre development at Tahawas is the largest source of titanium in the U.S. Other mineral products include talc, zinc, bauxite, salt, granite, marble, and a high grade of garnet used for abrasives.

There's a growing cottage industy for crafts, whether made from wood, metal or fabric, and this is becoming a consistent money maker for thousands of people.

Although the number of farms has declined in the Adirondacks, family farms still coexist along with large commercial enterprises. But weather conditions limit what can be grown commercially because the growing season is under 100 days a year. The region is a top producer of maple syrup and, on its periphery, there are extensive dairy farms and apple orchards.

I returned to the Adirondacks in 1994 after an absence of 50 years. I fully expected the tourist business would be booming, and it was, but the air of confidence expressed by all came as a surprise. At a time when my adopted state of California is in the depths of what seems to some like a near-depression, the Adirondacks are prospering, not just in tourism but in a wide variety of business enterprises. Most notable are the huge malls like those in Plattsburgh and Lake George village. Nothing in California can compare to them. Much of the area's new affluence stems from the North American Free Trade Agreement. Canadians now come by the tens of thousands to upstate New York, where almost everything can be bought far more cheaply than in Canada. Canadian business people are investing in the Adirondacks region. It is an area long known for its industrious, educated workers, and where cheap hydro-electric power sharply reduces the cost of doing business. Many satellite units of major U.S. corporations have also learned to appreciate the region's friendly business climate and have located in some of the local towns.

Adirondackers are a proud, self-reliant people with an exceptional heritage. Few areas anywhere in the world are as rich in natural beauty and in history as upstate New York. Almost every community has not one but several reminders of our republic's early formative years. Most have been lovingly preserved for this and future generations. Take the time to see them. I guarantee your visit will be a refreshing and heartwarming experience.

The Changing Seasons

The Adirondacks spring to life in April as winter's mantle of snow and ice begins to disappear under the relentless warmth of sun and rain, although lakes and streams are still rimmed with ice. It is a time when all living things step livelier with the promise of sunshiny days ahead now that the long, dreary isolation of winter has ended. By the third week of the month even the lakes and streams are free of ice. The soggy ground is soon covered with green shoots as long-dormant plants reach skyward for sustenance.

Traditionally this is the time when Adirondack housewives open wide their doors and windows to let the fresh breezes chase away the stagnant air of winter trapped in homes sealed tight with storm windows. For them, this is house-cleaning time and they bend to it with a will.

Brooks and rivers team with trout, rising in a cascade of color to snatch a bug from the air and occasionally a look-alike lure cast by an eager angler. Each year avid fishermen put their lives on hold for the annual ritual of the opening of the trout season in April. Few are successful, complaining as thousands have before them that the fish population is dying out. It is more likely that the spring rains have washed so many bugs and worms into the streams that the trout have more than they can eat.

In some years the rains stop coming in late April and then the most feared situation of all develops in the Adirondacks. This lovely land, by law consigned to be forever wild, is now a powder keg of tinder-dry growth.

But, when the rains fall regularly, abundant plant life flourishes. Trillium and jack-in-the-pulpit thrust their spears through the fresh humus deposited by plants and trees for thousands of years. Arbutus throng the sunnier spots along with dainty pink and yellow lady-slippers that brighten the ground with islands of loveliness.

Occasionally snow falls at night but each day's bright sun hastens its departure. Over this lush land birds swing effortlessly through the sky, their voices joyously heralding earth's rebirth from its frozen state. The first hawks wheel through the sky, as the hermit thrush, the vireo and the phoebe fill the air with songs. The thrush's voice is clear and flutelike, particularly at dawn and twilight.

Often called the American nightingale, the thrush's beautiful notes range high and low, before ending in a tremolo effect. Silent most of the time, and hidden by thick evergreen, the hermit thrush's brown monk's cowl, his rust-colored tail, and his spotted breast blend with fallen leaves as it searches for grubs.

The white-eyed vireo is a shy bird, making known its presence from within a tangled thicket with an outpouring of songs that end incongruously in a strong "chick." But his songs encompass a wide repertory: now a whine, next a mew, but with a variety of sounds in imitation of a host of other birds. If you happen to get too close, this green and white bird will stand his ground and scold you. The most brilliantly-colored of all vireos is the yellow-throated variety, with a bright yellow throat and breast. Its distinctive voice is rich and full.

Phoebes are a joy to watch as, darting from their perches beside a mountain stream, with unfailing accuracy they snatch a bug in flight. Somewhat drab, most phoebes are brown and gray. Not known for their musical prowess, the eastern phoebes can be recognized by their familiar call "fee-bee."

More color creeps into the countryside in May with the pale scarlet of the maple, the light green of the birches and the pale yellow of the tamarack. Some years unusually warm weather hastens nature's timetable and the color seems to leap out of the forest overnight.

The poplar is the most despised tree in the Adirondacks because its wood is brittle and of little use for anything. But this month, as if to make up for its shortcomings, it puts on a display that makes it the loveliest sight in the woods. Its fringed catkins, with gold-green and yellow-green fuzzy-looking flowers, dominate the woods even at a distance with their flashes of green and yellow light. Its glory lasts but a brief time and it is soon overshadowed by birches and maples. Meanwhile, the last of the winter's snow glistens on the mountain peaks. It, too, will soon disappear, although night-time temperatures often drop to the mid-30s. Alpine flowers spread their delicate carpets of color as the snow recedes.

The flowers that bloom in May are everywhere, including the white shadbush, which is the first to bloom, followed by the wild cherry's white blooms. The buds of the spruce and tamarack now turn blue-green, as do the scotch pines along roadsides.

The woods come alive with birds. Black poll warblers arrive after most other birds have settled in the Adirondacks from their wintering days in South America. The male sings happily while the female makes a nest for their eggs. His black crown is streaked with gray down his back. His cheeks and wing bars are white, as is his underside. In the fall, the male and female and their young have greenish underparts, yellowish breasts and wing bars. Wood peewees are not far behind them, filling the woods with their sweet, plaintive "pee-a-wee-peaas." These gray-brown birds are unobtrusive, and their calls seem to come out of nowhere like a disembodied voice. But in the early morning and at dusk the peewee varies his phrases so that they take on the semblance of a charming song. But the true harbinger of spring is a lovely bird with a brick-red chest, a charcoal-gray coat and a black head. The robin's "cheerily, cheerily, cheerily" brings a smile to people's faces as it hops or runs across a grassy expanse, cocks his head, and then stabs the ground with his beak. Up comes an unwilling grub or worm.

High in the sky gulls float over the woods after flying from nearby Lake Champlain. Their raucous cries blend with the harsh "caw-caw" of crows while the loon's haunting cry from some nearby lake adds a further touch of otherworldliness. Although most ducks have headed for the far north, here and there a few black ducks settle down on a remote pond or lake for the summer.

Throughout the Adirondacks boats are launched on a favorite remote lake by fishermen who repeat an age-old ritual year-after-year.

If this sounds idyllic, it is marred somewhat by black flies that can drive you almost frantic. Their bite, like that of the mosquito and the punkie, can be annoying and somewhat painful. They are a menace throughout the day, but even worse at dawn and dusk when the fishing is at its best. Hordes of these persistent bugs will chase a deer, causing it to run frantically for the nearest pond to gain relief by immersing itself.

At May's end the flowers in the Adirondacks reach their peak of loveliness, often scenting the air. Every farmhouse and cabin seems to be surrounded by a riot of lilac in full bloom. These are the old-fashioned lavender-blue types and not the newer varieties cultivated by nurseries. They have bloomed for years and some clumps are more than 20 feet wide. They put on displays of color that have to be seen to be appreciated. In the last 50 years tens of thousands of homesteads have been abandoned because of the harshness of the winters and the short growing season, which makes it impossible to earn a living by growing agricultural products. Although thousands of abandoned homes and barns remain as testament to failed dreams, the lilacs remain to testify that some things are eternal.

Around most abandoned farms are gnarled apple trees, some with only a few blossoms on limbs that still experience the rise of sap. Each year they fight off the savage winters and attempt to make it through the summer, offering a feast to birds and animals.

The month of May comes to an end but in sun-lit areas little pink bells signify that in a couple of months avid blueberry pickers will throng the woods, filling gallon pails with luscious berries.

June is the month when the Adirondacks takes on varying shades of green as plants and trees expand their canopies with new growth. With rising temperatures, a haze floats over hill and dale that only four months earlier were gaunt and barren and covered by snow. Some nights can be hot and windless, bringing out the bugs in incredible numbers. There is a breathless feel to the air that sets water beetles whirling like mad dervishes on ponds and steams. These are nights when wise Adirondackers remain indoors behind screened windows. Such is the nature of the land, however, that some nights in early June frost settles on the ground, although it quickly disappears with the rising sun.

Mornings are enlivened by kingfishers hovering over a stretch of clear water. Suddenly, from a height of 50 feet, the kingfisher starts his dive into the water, his strong beak and back absorbing the shock as he emerges with a fingerling in his beak. He flies to a high tree branch and stuns the fish by cracking its head against the bough. Then he flips it into the air and catches it head first. One gulp and the small fish disappears. The belted kingfisher is the most common in the Adirondacks, with its blue-gray back and chest band and with white belly feathers. Normally the kingfisher stakes out an area and chases away intruders with its harsh, grating call.

In nearby trees gaudy woodpeckers, with their bright red crests and white-splashed black wings, set up a racket that must be heard to be believed. They use their sharp beaks to dig out tree-boring grubs and to hollow out a place inside a dead tree for a nest.

Those unfamiliar with the whims of nature here should take heed when a mountain thunderstorm rumbles in the distance. Those in canoes or small boats should anticipate the violent impact of the storm's strong winds and head for shore. A pond or lake can be whipped into a froth of white and violently toss a boat's occupants into the water.

In June Adirondackers prepare for the annual invasion of city folk. They come up by the thousands, some seeking a quiet vacation, while others head for the mountain slopes' well-marked trails. Children throng lake shores, marveling about the incredible beauty of a land little changed since the Europeans began to colonize eastern America in the 17th Century. This "getting back" to nature restores tired minds and bodies of young and old alike, giving them a renewed sense of the magnificence of a largely undeveloped land.

In July some areas are a riot of color as summer flowers burst into bloom, and there is a strong scent of fresh pine in the air. Now the weather becomes even more unpredictable, with hot nights followed by temperatures that dip briefly below freezing. Prolonged droughts raise the fire danger.

With the opening of the bass season on the 3rd Saturday in June, lasting through November 30, anglers head for the thousands of lakes to try their luck with the small mouth bass. Purists scorn others who use live bait, although their expensive lures often prove equally unsuccessful. Pound-for-pound the small mouth bass ranks with the scrappiest of all game fish. Whatever the bait, it strikes hard, rising angrily out of the water in shocked surprise when it finds a metal hook in its mouth. With a light rod and line, the battle can be long and thrilling, and even experienced anglers marvel at the determination of this small fish, averaging three to five pounds, to remain alive and free. Its succulence rivals any fish caught in the Adirondacks. Its meaty sides separate easily from its bones. Although old-timers have their favorite "holes" that they religiously guard at dusk and dawn, bass can be elusive, seldom appearing the same place on a given day. But that is the challenge that draws anglers year after year to remote lakes in the Adirondacks. The heavenly bliss of a beautiful lake, whose stillness is broken only occasionally by the cry of a loon, is one that should be experienced by every human being, fisherman or not. You will come as close to perfect peace of mind as a human being can get.

For those seeking privacy, July in the Adirondacks should be avoided. It is jammed with people, while power boats cruise the larger lakes, adding to the cacophony of sounds made by thousands of people bent on getting the maximum enjoyment out of their two weeks in the "woods." State camps are filled to capacity, with hundreds of fireplaces alight at night as campers prepare the canned food they've brought with them. Many places begin to resemble the crowded cities from whence these hordes of people have come.

Here and there sunlit meadows attract deer and bear in search of luscious blueberries and raspberries. Those who would harvest these berries in late July and early August may find they have competition. Caution is advised. Blueberries grow mostly on low bushes in accessible areas, but raspberries are in tangled thickets that try one's patience.

August's weather can be unpredictable – hot one day, cold the next. Now a few maple leaves show the first signs of scarlet, heralding the fact that summer is fleeting and fall and winter are not far behind. Crickets seem louder; their chirpings rising to a chorus that fills the night air.

By now most of the children's camps are closed, and the Adirondackers breathe a sigh of relief as their communities settle down to a more normal pace. Hotels are still crowded but their older occupants are a more subdued lot seeking primarily peace and quiet. The woods still display their beauty as late flowers brighten fields and roadsides with Queen Ann's lace, wild asters and phlox.

By September most of the tourists have departed for distant homes like the migrating birds who have flown south in flock. Grosbeaks still linger, although the male has lost most of his brilliant breast feathers. These large-beaked birds feast on animal and vegetable matter, particularly wild fruit. The male's rich, melodic voice rises suddenly in the woods, charming everyone with its beauty. After Labor Day few visitors are still around to enjoy two of the best months of the Adirondack year – September and October. With noisy visitors gone, deer and other large animals return to the shores of the lakes from which they were driven during the summer months. They soon will flee again to the deep recesses of the forest when the hunting season opens in October.

Now the colors of the deciduous trees begin to turn and some, like the sugar maple, are resplendent with multi-hued colors before they wither and carpet the ground with a torrent of color. Only those who have seen this fall coloring can appreciate its incredible beauty, spreading for hundreds of miles in every direction. The first frost, usually around September 15, but often earlier, hastens the process. Sunsets in the clear atmosphere of fall are spectacular and of almost unbelievable intensity. With a severe frost occurring almost daily as the month comes to an end, the mountain peaks glisten whitely.

In most years the peak of the fall coloring is reached in early October and the forest shines vividly in every variety of red known to man. Some have counted 50 different shades. When only a few maples are surrounded by pine and spruce trees, they seem to catch fire. With the sun sinking in the west, the red turns to purple against a background of a gold sky. People travel from near and far just to see the fall coloring. Some years, due to inadequate rainfall and erratic frosts, the spectacle loses some of its drama but even then it is a sight to behold.

Walks in the woods during October are like walking through a beautiful cathedral and one feels awed by the effect. But the scene fades in a few days and the deciduous trees, minus their brilliant plumage, stand stark and naked. The woods become oddly quiet now that the last of the migrant song birds have departed. Much of the forest, stripped of its leaves, has a gaunt look. The Adirondacks are not a major flyway, but geese and ducks occasionally are seen in their tight "V" formations. Now is the time for hunters to don their scarlet jackets and search the woods for grouse and woodcock. Grouse hide in thick woods. They especially like old apple orchards with their rotting fruit. Eight or 10 birds can often be found under such circumstances, and the flight of a single grouse can startle hunters with the strongest nerves. They make an incredible racket considering their size. Woodcocks are found in swampy areas or around old pastures. These elusive birds are rarely seen unless one has a trained bird dog.

The regular hunting season for deer and bear begins October 23 and lasts until December 5. This is the time of year when local residents are particularly careful in the woods, knowing from sad experience that inept hunters of big game are apt to shoot at anything that moves. When the first shot is fired, deer and bear that only a few weeks earlier had been seen around habitations leave for the most secluded parts of the forest. Such hunting requires skill and patience. The thousands of men and women thrashing through the woods can be heard for miles so it's no wonder that many hunters never see a deer or bear, although it is calculated that in some years more than 200,000 deer are taken throughout the state. Experienced hunters hope for snow to make it easier to track deer. Certainly walking in snow reduces the noise one makes over a thick layer of leaves. Those who hunt in groups are most successful. Deer tend to go into swamps and other low places at night to feed. With dawn, wise hunters line the ridges around such places, carefully watching the obvious runways. Drives are made to windward, with the thought that the deer will be chased towards the rifles of their friends.

Snow flurries are common with the coming of November. If it is an otherwise dry fall, Adirondackers cast anxious eyes at the least sign of a smoky haze in the distance, even those from Canada. When the haze becomes so intense that it dims the sun they carefully review evacuation plans. But most days are gray, with thick cloud cover and there is a chill in the air. Ice forms along the edges of the lakes. If a severe drought continues, the woods are closed and all hunters are ordered out. But this is an unusual situation. If the worst materializes, a small army of forest rangers bears down on fires and soon snuffs them out.

The early snows in November give way to heavier downfalls in December and Adirondackers settle down in their houses and await the coming of spring. Now the lakes are frozen solid, with frigid temperatures occasionally reaching 52° below zero. Tiny tracks to and from a lake shore indicate that a mink or muskrat is seemingly oblivious to the temperature.

The leaden skies of December occasionally give way to brilliant sunshine that, reflected off the deep snow, stabs painfully at unprotected eyes. Now it is man against nature, and the wise man or woman remains within snug walls. The automobile, such a necessary means of conveyance the rest of the year, now becomes a snowbound monster incapable of movement after heavy snow. Sometimes it falls continuously night and day until at least 15 inches, possibly more, have brought everything to a standstill. Snowplows eventually open the roads for automobiles but travel by foot often is quicker.

Now a new round of visitors make their appearance as skiers descend on the Adirondacks in growing numbers. Except for skilifts, the woods are left to the animals. During a particularly bad winter of heavy snowfalls, deer die of starvation by the thousands, each trapped in a small circle of trampled ground, having sought in vain for tender shoots to sustain them. For the hardy men and women who trek through the woods on foot at this time of year it is an enchanted, sparkling world inhabited by raucous blue jays, white-breasted nuthatches and chickadees. Hunters seek the snowshoe rabbit, and they are often successful because the animals are so easy to track. Their "footprints" are 12 inches across, indicating where their whole body has rested.

Adirondack towns are alive with young people during the holiday season as they come to the mountains by the thousands. In the crisp, cold air mountain peaks sparkle under the influence of the sun. For those who love to ski, and they are counted in the millions, the Adirondacks are a godsend. Easily accessible by AMTRAK trains from New York City and Montreal, skiing areas have become increasingly popular. A few forego the ski trails and climb the mountains, despite conditions that try men's souls.

With the dawning of a new year the Adirondack nights remain clear and cold. Now grosbeaks and other over-wintering birds gratefully accept the largesse of feeding stations in backyards. These birds, with their thick parrot-like yellow-green beaks, first appeared in numbers in the late 19th Century and they have increased ever since. Tropical looking, they often range up to eight inches long and seem out of place in this frigid landscape. The male is yellow-gold and black with white patches on his wings, while the female is much less brightly colored with gray tones.

Although lakes and ponds are frozen solid a large band of intrepid fisherman can be found at dawn each day chopping two holes in a foot of ice – sometimes more – to fish for trout. Despite bitter cold and winds that seem to penetrate the warmest clothing, these men and women sit or stand for hours over these holes. The luckier ones have shanties to help shield them.

January is a deceptive time in the Adirondacks. Bitter cold throughout much of the month, there's often a warm spell at mid-month generated by a south wind. The snow starts to recede, but this is only temporary. Winter has not had its last fling, but to residents this period is a welcome relief.

February can be an exasperating month with its frequent snow storms, usually not much at one time, but a relentless warning that it is still winter in the Adirondacks. It is the coldest month of all and mornings of 25 or 30° below zero are common. Daylight hours remain bright and sunny and sunsets cast a purple hue that tints the snow. The prairie horned larks are the first of the migratory birds to return to the woods after spending the previous months in the South. These chocolate-colored birds are larger than sparrows with two black tufts like horns on their head and a straight claw protruding on the back of each leg. They roam the meadows, where the snow has thawed or blown away, searching for seeds. They never roost in trees, preferring the ground, where they start to build nests in a snow-free spot. Oftentimes a snowfall will bury their nest, but the female just builds another and lays her eggs. These early birds often raise three or four broods of young before they head south in autumn. They fill their drab surroundings with song. There is no beauty to their singing but their songs are so unusual at this time of year that one forgets their lack of melodic appeal.

About all that can be said for March is that one should look for the unexpected. Low temperatures alternate with periods of above-freezing temperatures that leave the snow mottled and dirty, all its pristine whiteness a thing of the past. So changeable is the weather that a day can start with a warm south wind which in a few hours becomes a cold north wind that chills the bones, before it changes back to the south. This is "sugar weather" or bright sunny days that start the sap flowing upward in the maple trees after cold, crisp nights. New taps are made in the trees, buckets hung, and gatherers hope for the best. If this is a good year, huge kettles of sap will soon be boiling over outdoor wood fires to reduce the sap to the consistency of maple syrup. By March 20 sugaring is usually over for the year.

The Adirondack Region

Now the swelling buds of the maples, and many other trees, provide a sure sign that spring is on the way. Robins are back, but sometimes they get caught in a late snow and are forced with other birds to seek shelter from the elements. Adirondackers watch for the first sign of a south wind, knowing it often will bring a warm rain to wash away the last of the snow. Now there is the sound of running water in most places as streams free themselves from their icy embrace to flow freely. With the earth's release from frost, the ground becomes soggy but full of emerging plant life that deer nibble hungrily, with the surviving fawns born the previous month trying unsteadily to keep up with their mothers. The bears now leave their dens where they have slept the winter away and where the females gave birth to cubs now gazing wide-eyed at this new world.

The Adirondack Park

The Adirondacks is like nowhere else in the United States and no national park is as large. In 1894 the Adirondack Forest Preserve was protected by an amendment to the state constitution providing that it "shall be forever kept as wild forest lands." This "forever wild" law can be altered only by an amendment voted on by all citizens of the state. Several attempts have been made but all have failed.

The Adirondack State Park was established in 1892 and a blue line was used on an official map to establish its boundaries. This "blue line" was redrawn in 1929 to include some parcels on the west shore of Lake Champlain and on both sides of Lake George.

Originally it was hoped that the park would include all privately owned land but this proved unrealistic because villages and cities could not be purchased and many private owners refused to sell. Therefore the "blue line" marked the boundaries of the state park but the five and a half million acres of the territory enclosed in it is only half owned by the state. The actual figure is 2,243,170 acres. Therefore the park is a checkerboard of small and large parcels owned by private investors and the state. State-owned sections may not be "leased, sold, or exchanged, nor shall the timber there be sold, removed, or destroyed." Private parcels have few restrictions and may be sold or traded. The park is a rough rectangle with 120 miles on each side. There are a number of high peaks in the center but Mt. Marcy is the tallest at 5,344 feet. In the northeast and northwest the mountainous slopes change to rolling hill country with broad plateaus. There are 46 peaks higher than 4,000 feet and these "high peaks" are clustered within a 50-square-mile area.

Adirondack Auto Trails

In 1927 a road was started up Whiteface Mountain for automobiles. Its construction was fought by most conservation groups but, for those unable or disinclined to climb the mountain, its view of the Adirondacks on a clear day is spectacular. From its summit one can see many of the 1,345 lakes. In the southwest quarter of the park many of these lakes are inter-connected and one can canoe through them for 100 miles. The highest lake is the most northerly source of the Hudson River. Lake George is the largest lake wholly within the "blue line." Although the park reaches a few points on Lake Champlain, this lake is not considered part of it.

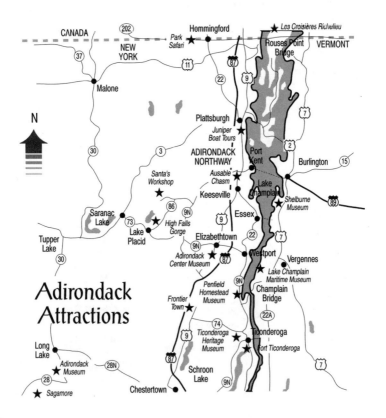

The once venerable forests were largely gone by 1920, with less than 4% of the forest preserve remaining as virgin timber. The destructive hurricane that hit the region in 1950 was particularly devastating to stands of big trees. There are still big trees in the park but most are second growth timber, some dating back 100 years. White pines are subject to a blight called "blister rust" that seems to be present when wild currents or gooseberries are growing nearby. The latter are destroyed wherever they are found.

The final section of the Northway (I-87) to the Canadian border was completed in the spring of 1967, opening the region's incredible beauty to additional vacationers. Despite opposition by conservationists, the Northway was approved along a route that did minimal damage to the environment. The old two-lane Route 9 had long outlived its usefulness and had become a danger to all who used it.

During the later part of the 19th Century the Adirondacks became fashionable for summer tourists and huge hotels were built to provide them with the best accommodations in the region. These old inns and hotels were really a reflection of the men who created them but their wooden construction doomed most of them to destruction by fire. Automobiles eventually killed off those that remained. The era of the great Adirondack hotels ended in 1962 when Saranac Inn closed its doors.

Access Routes

The Adirondacks extend to Lake Champlain on the east while the Mohawk and St. Lawrence valleys mark the southern and northern limits. The best access to the mountainous interior is to take the Northway (I-87) and get off at either 9N/86 or 73. From the Thruway (I-90) that crosses the state's central section, take State Routes 30 and 12/28.

Adirondack Museum. This replica of an early hotel in the Adirondacks is one of an incredible assortment of buildings and displays here on the shores of Blue Mountain Lake.

State Routes 9N/86 and 73 are winding roads that pass through 50 miles of small farms, resort communities and some of the most beautiful mountain country you'll encounter anywhere. The roads merge near Lake Placid. Nearby is Wilmington, where 4,867-foot Whiteface Mountain rears skyward. It is the highest skiing peak in the East and you can drive up it, weather permitting. West of Lake Placid is the town of Saranac Lake.

The other principal routes into the Adirondacks start at the Thru-way (I-90). State Route 30 leaves I-90 near Amsterdam and State Route 12/28 from I-90 near Utica. The **Adirondack Museum** is located here and gives a thorough background on the region. At the **Adirondack Lakes Center for the Arts**, summer concerts are held each year. The scenery gets even more spectacular along Route 30 to Raquette Lake and the town of **Tupper Lake**. During the 19th Century, industrialists built huge camps all through this area as hunting lodges. The town began as a lumber and sawmill village in the 1890s. There are excellent fishing, swimming and boating opportunities at Big Tupper Lake, Lake Simond, the Raquette River and Raquette Pond. They are all easily reached from Tupper Lake.

For Canadians who live west of Montreal, there is a good access road via State Route 30 that goes south through Malone, New York from Huntingdon, Canada. It connects with roads to all three of the Tri-Lakes areas in the central Adirondacks – Lake Placid, Saranac Lake and Tupper Lake. Most of the route is highly scenic.

Travelers from the west might consider the alternate route into the Adirondacks from Watertown – Route 3. I-91 connects with the Thruway at Syracuse. Most of it is highly scenic. The route ends in the Tri-Lakes region described above.

For travelers on limited time schedules, or those who don't wish to drive to the Adirondacks, Albany Airport is served by most major domestic airlines including American, Delta, Continental Express, Northwest, Transworld, United and USAIR.

For passengers seeking to fly to Plattsburgh, Lake Placid or Saranac Lake from Albany, USAIR has daily service.

Lake Champlain

L ake Champlain lies in the foothills of the Adirondacks. It is cleaner than any other lake its size and is crystal clear. For those who love to sail, fish, swim or just look at magnificent scenery, Lake Champlain is unsurpassed.

Just below the Canadian border and right off the Adirondack Northway (I-87) lies Clinton County whose eastern border is Lake Champlain. It is only 60 miles south of Montreal in Canada and 160 miles north of Albany. Year-round, it's a recreational playground for a variety of activities.

About 500 million years ago the earth's crust crumpled and created a gaping valley alongside one of the oldest mountain ranges on earth. This upheaval also formed the mountain ranges to the east – the Green Mountains of Vermont. This huge gap in the earth was later filled by the earth's developing oceans and became what is now known as Lake Champlain.

It covers an area of approximately 490 square miles, making it the sixth largest body of fresh water in the United States. It is 107 miles long, 12 miles wide across its widest point and has a maximum depth of 399 feet. Its waters flow north from Whitehall, New York, draining eventually into the St. Lawrence River through the Richelieu River in Quebec, Canada.

Lake Champlain has its own version of Scotland's Loch Ness monster called "Champ." It was first reported by Samuel de Champlain in 1609, who wrote that he saw a serpentine creature 20 feet long, as thick as a barge and with the head of a horse. Sightings are still reported but no one has ever gotten a picture to prove such a creature exists.

You can explore this historic lake from the deck of a cruise boat. On the enclosed, all-steel, twin diesel-powered *Jupiter* you can see historic **Valcour Island** with its scenic shoreline, the Adirondacks to the west and the Green Mountains to the east providing a majestic backdrop. The Battle of Valcour, the first naval engagement of the Revolutionary War, was fought between the island and the New York shore.

Visit **Crab Island**, where there's a monument commemorating the Battle of Plattsburgh in 1814. To the west is the historic **Hotel Champlain**, now Clinton County Community College. It was once used by several presidents as a summer White House.

Upon your return you will cruise by the site of Commodore Macdonough's victory over a British fleet in 1814 that effectively ended the War of 1812. This day cruise leaves at 1 p.m., May to September, from the foot of Dock Street at Plattsburgh Harbor. There's a night cruise during this same period that leaves at 6 p.m. and returns four hours later, billed as a "Steak 'N Sunset Cruise." Along with the excellent food there is dancing under the stars. Locally you can call 561-8970 for information and reservations or toll-free 1-800-388-8970.

At the New York end of the Lake Champlain Bridge is a monument erected by the State of New York and Vermont to honor Samuel de Champlain, who discovered the lake in 1609 that now bears his name. Auguste Rodin sculpted the bas relief **"La France"** as a gift from that country in 1909. It is located seven and a half miles northeast on State Route 8. The Lake Champlain fleet and colonial armies used this region as a staging area for battles fought further north. It is open from 11 a.m. to 7 p.m. and Sunday-Tuesday 11 a.m. to 4 p.m. from Memorial Day to Labor Day. Camping and picnicking are permitted and the admission is $3. For information call (518) 891-1370.

On this same site are the preserved remains of fortifications occupied during the French and Indian and Revolutionary wars. There's a visitor center to recount the history of the area and its archaeology, with emphasis on the 1734 French **Fort St. Frédéric** and the 1769 British fort **Crown Point**. There are self-guided tours Wednesday-Saturday from 10 a.m. to 5 p.m., late May to late October. There is no admission. For further details, call (518) 597-3666.

The most interesting and noteworthy historic site is **Fort Ticonderoga**. It's a mile northeast of the village of Ticonderoga on State Route 74. The French built it in 1755 on a promontory facing Lake Champlain and named it Fort Carillon. It was positioned to control the connecting waterway between Canada and the American colonies. The British tried to capture the fort in 1758 but failed. The following year British General Jeffrey Amherst did take it. He rebuilt the fort and changed its name to Fort Ticonderoga.

In 1775 Ethan Allen and his Green Mountain Boys captured the fort in a surprise attack without casualties on either side. Benedict

Fort Ticonderoga. Aerial view of the fort today.

Arnold assembled a small fleet here in 1776 and used it to delay a much larger British fleet. General John Burgoyne captured the fort for the British but later that year it was abandoned after his defeat at Saratoga. The buildings were burned on both sides of the lake and the fort was never garrisoned again.

Fort Ticonderoga has been restored on its original foundations according to the original French plans. Memorabilia from the colonial and Revolutionary War periods are on display in the museum. The battleground surrounding the fort where the French under the Marquis de Montcalm defeated British and colonial troops in 1758 is precisely marked so you can understand the battle.

Mount Defiance, where the British hauled cannon to the summit and forced General St. Clair to surrender the American-held fort in 1777, is one mile southeast off State Route 22/24. There's a black-top road up it now over some of the route the British used to haul their cannon. From an overlook you get a panoramic view of Lake

Champlain and the Green Mountains in Vermont. The route is open 9 a.m. to 5 p.m. during July and August and from 9 a.m. to 4 p.m., May 10 to June 30, and again from September 1 to October 18. There is no charge.

History cruises on Lake Champlain are made by the **NV Carillon**, covering Ticonderoga, Mount Independence and Hand's Cove. During the last week in June there's a French and Indian War re-enactment and encampment. Guided tours are offered from July through August with cannon firing and drum music. Bagpipers compete on July 9 in the International Piping Contest.

Fort Ticonderoga is open daily 9 a.m. to 6 p.m., July to August, 9 a.m. to 5 p.m., May 10 to June 30 and September 1 to October 18. Admission is $7, but $6.30 for people 62 and over. For ages 10-13 the admission is $5. For further details call (518) 585-2821.

Ferries

There are three ferry systems that make the crossing of Lake Champlain to and from New York and Vermont. Between Plattsburgh and Grand Isle, Vermont, the first departure from Grand Isle is at 7:40 a.m. and from Plattsburgh at 8 a.m. They maintain a schedule every 20 minutes. The last departure from Plattsburgh is at 9:20 p.m. and the final one from Grand Isle is 9 p.m. On major holidays departures take place every 40 minutes. Times vary due to traffic or icy conditions in the winter. To reach the ferry terminal in Vermont take Interstate 89 and use Exit 17. Then drive 12 miles to the ferry. From New York, take Interstate 87 and get off at Exit 39. It is five miles from there to the ferry. The rate one way for a car and driver is $6.75 and the round trip costs $10.75. For an adult passenger the one-way rate is $1.75 and $2.50 for the round trip. The ferry ride takes 12 minutes.

The ferry from Burlington, Vermont to Port Kent, New York has three different schedules. In the summer, from June 24-September 6, the ferry's first departure from Burlington is at 7:15 a.m. and the

Lake Champlain ferries. The Vermont, in the foreground, was built in 1992. The older ferry dates back to 1913.

first from Port Kent is at 9:30 a.m. Burlington's last ferry in the summer leaves at 7:45 p.m. and from Port Kent at 9 p.m. In spring, the first ferry leaves Burlington at 5:30 p.m. and 6:30 p.m. from Port Kent. In the fall, from September 7-October 17, the first ferry leaves Burlington at 8 a.m. and 9:20 from Port Kent. The last ferry leaves Burlington at 5:30 p.m. and Port Kent at 6:30 p.m. The crossing takes an hour. To reach the Vermont ferry terminal, drive Interstate 89 and take Exit 15W. Another two miles will get you to the terminal. From New York, take Interstate 87, and make your exit at 34 or 35, then drive another six miles to the ferry. The rate for a one-way trip with a car and driver is $12 and $21 for a round trip. Each other adult passenger is charged $3 one way and $6.50 for a round trip. For children six through 12 the one-way rate is $1 and $1.50 for a round trip. Children under six travel free. The maximum car fare is $19 one way and $28 for a round trip. From Charlotte, Vermont to Essex, New York the summer schedule (May 20-October 24) starts at 6:30 a.m. from Charlotte and 7:00 a.m. from

Essex. The last ferry leaves Charlotte at 9:30 p.m. and 10 p.m. from Essex.

The spring schedule from April 1-May 15, and the fall schedule from October 25-January 2, starts at 6:30 a.m. from Charlotte and 7 a.m. from Essex. The last ferry leaves Charlotte at 6 p.m. and from Essex at 6:30 p.m. Please note that the April 1 opening is subject to icy conditions, and all late fall and winter departures may be disrupted by weather conditions. The crossing time is 20 minutes. On this ferry there's an overhead clearance of 13.6 feet. To reach the Charlotte ferry terminal on U.S. 7 take Route F-5 at Charlotte and drive three miles to the ferry. From the New York side, take Interstate 87 and use Exits 31 or 33; it is 12 miles more to the ferry. The rate for a one-way car and driver is $6.75 and $10.75 for a round trip. Each adult passenger must pay $1.75 for one way and $2.50 for a round trip. Children six to 12 are charged $.50 for a one-way ticket and $.75 for a round trip. Children under six ride free. The maximum car fare is $11.25 one way and $17 for a round trip.

These ferries are owned by the Lake Champlain Transportation Company, King Street Dock, Burlington, Vermont 05401. They've been in business since 1826. Their 10-ship fleet includes the *Adirondack*, the oldest ferry in the country, and the newest (the *Vermont*), placed in service in 1992. If you're on a tight schedule, or traveling on a holiday, it would be wise to check on these schedules by calling (802) 864-9804.

Near the small village of Essex on Lake Champlain there's a place called **Split Rock**. According to Indian legends tribal members threw gifts into the water to appease whatever evil spirits congregated there, thus assuring a safe passage. Dutchman Arent Van Curler, who founded Schenectady, ignored the warnings of his Indian allies that he must pay homage to the Indian chief's spirit who dwelt there. His canoe capsized and he was drowned. Essex is on Route 22 today so take heed if you pass Split Rock. The old chief's spirit may still be lingering there.

Other than those noted for Plattsburgh, there are no recommended places to stay or to eat on the lake. There are, however, excellent establishments within an hour's drive from any point on the lake that will be far more satisfactory and often cheaper.

Plattsburgh

Plattsburgh is outside the Adirondack Park but it is within an easy drive of most scenic areas.

The **Macdonough Monument**, built in 1926, commemorates Commodore Macdonough's victory over the British fleet in Cumberland Bay during the War of 1812. This was the final decisive naval battle between the Americans and the British on September 11, 1814. The monument is open only a few times during the year to the public. Call the Clinton County Historical Association at 561-0340 for the dates of the monument's openings .

The **Champlain Monument** in River Walk Park was a gift from France in 1909 celebrating the 300th anniversary of Samuel de Champlain's discovery of Lake Champlain. President William Howard Taft and many dignitaries from France were present for the dedication.

The **Kent-Delord House Museum** in Plattsburgh is linked with some of the most important and significant events in our country's infancy. The house was built in 1797. It was commandeered as the British headquarters in 1814 during the Battle of Plattsburgh. Tours are held Tuesday through Saturday at 12:00 noon, 1:30 p.m. and 3:00 p.m. Call 561-1035 for further information.

In the vicinity of Plattsburgh there are three excellent state parks. **Point Au Roche** is one of the newest, located on the north-western shore of Lake Champlain. It's a mixture of open and forested land, with the majority underdeveloped and natural.

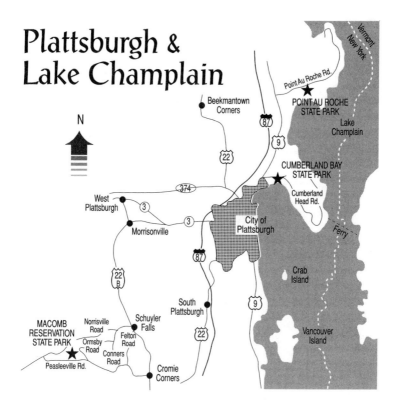

Plattsburgh & Lake Champlain

The park also has a large day-use area with a long, protected sandy beach, a picnic area and a concession stand. There is also a staffed nature center with trails which offer a variety of interesting habitats. The trails are used all year for school programs, general nature hikes and cross-country skiing.

Cumberland Bay State Park is located on the northwest shore of Lake Champlain. Many of the buildings and beach improvements were built by the Civilian Conservation Corps during the administration of President Franklin D. Roosevelt. Members of the corps developed the marsh-and-sand-dune areas which constitute 2,700 feet of lake front. It is now a modern, up-to-date state campsite, a large picnic area and a beautiful sandy beach.

Macomb Recreation State Park is the third park in the Lake Champlain park complex. It is outside the northeast corner of the Adirondack Park at Schuyler Falls. The large parcels of state land that surround the facility give it a wilderness feel. Man-made Davis Pond is used for non-motorized boats and for swimming. A large picnic area offers a place to enjoy the pond and the wooded area surrounding it. The pond can be fished but the Salmon River offers better opportunities, not only for fishing but for swimming. Lake Champlain and the Adirondacks are nearby for those who wish to take day trips to them.

Where to Stay

Comfort Inn can be reached by taking Exit 37 from I-87. It offers a senior discount and some indoor/outdoor activities, and it has its own restaurant. From 5/1-10/31 the rate is $69-$78. For reservations, write the Inn at 495 Cornelia Street, 12901, or call (518) 562-2730.

Holiday Inn is at the junction of I-87 and Exit 37. It offers a senior discount for its 102 units. From 6/18-9/4 the rate is $76-$86. From 9/5-10/17 the rate is $66-$76. From 10/18-12/31, the rate is $56-$66.

Where to Dine

Anthony's Restaurant is west of the junction of I-87, Exit 37, at 620 Upper Cornelia Street. It is open from 11:30 a.m.-2:30 p.m. and 5 p.m. to 9 p.m. except on major holidays. It serves continental food. For reservations, call (518) 561-6420.

Valcour Lodge on Lake Champlain is six and a quarter miles south of Plattsburgh on U.S. 9. From I-87, Exit 35, drive three miles east of U.S. 9, then three miles to the north. It's a steak and seafood restaurant on the lake, open 4/20-10/7 from 5 p.m. until 10 p.m. The lodge serves a Sunday buffet from 10 a.m. until 2 p.m.

Chazy

The village of **Chazy**, 12 miles north of Plattsburgh, is 300 years old. The **Alice T. Miner home**, constructed in 1824, is now a museum with a fabulous colonial collection. It contains many old, rare pieces of furniture and a diverse assortment of pewter, brass, silver and china as well as other forms of artwork. It is open Tuesday-Saturday from 10 a.m. to 4 p.m. Call 846-7336 for information.

There are no recommended places to stay or to eat in Chazy.

Peru

Every September the Town of Peru gathers for its annual **Apple Festival**. This whole area is "apple" country and most well-known varieties are produced, along with some that are little known elsewhere. There's an hour-long parade starting at 12 noon on the school grounds plus entertainment, including games, rides, bake sales, craft tables, drawings and raffles. Call 643-2435 for precise details.

There are no recommended places to stay or to eat in Peru.

Lake Placid

The village of Lake Placid is on the shores of Mirror Lake and Lake Placid. The village played host to the 1932 and 1980 Winter Olympics. Eight miles to the north there's downhill skiing at Whiteface

Mountain. Recreational activities of many varieties are available at both state and private facilities.

In summertime, bridle paths and bike paths take you through some of the most beautiful scenery you'll find in any mountain region. Private and public beaches, tennis courts, six golf courses, boating, and hiking trails await the more physically inclined. There is even summer ice skating in the Olympic Arena. On nearby Whiteface Mountain there are chairlift rides over grassy ski slopes, and the Whiteface Mountain Veterans' Memorial Highway will take you in comfort almost to the summit.

Two miles to the south on State Route 73, and three-quarters of a mile south on John Brown Road, is **John Brown Farm State Historic Site**. There's a monument marking the burial of the well-known abolitionist. It is open throughout the year and the self-guiding trails take about half an hour. A restored farmhouse is open Wednesday-Saturday from 10 a.m. to 5 p.m. and from late May until late October. It is also open on Memorial Day, July 4, Labor Day and October 4. Admission is free.

Boat rides on Mirror Lake in Lake Placid are available at the Marina a mile north of Mirror Lake Drive. These hour-long cruises are narrated and start daily at 10:30 a.m., 1 p.m., 2:30 p.m. and 4 p.m., June 24-Labor Day; mid-May to June 23 at 10:45 a.m., 1:30 p.m., 3 p.m. and the day after Labor Day-October 20. The fare is $6, but a dollar less for those over 65, and $4 for ages 3-12. For information, call (518) 523-9704.

Lake Placid's history is chronicled over the last 200 years at the **Lake Placid/North Elba Historical Society Museum**. It is two blocks from State Routes 73 and 86 on Averyville Road. Housed in a former railroad station, it is open Tuesday-Sunday from noon until 4 p.m., June-September. Admission is $1.

Two-and-a-half-hour sightseeing tours depart from all major hotels and motels in Lake Placid. Local historic and Olympic sites are visited and the fare includes admission into the Intervale Ski Jumping Complex. Tours depart Monday-Saturday at 9 a.m. and 1:30 p.m. and on Sunday at 1:30 p.m. They are run from Memorial Day weekend to October 31. They leave daily at 11 a.m. the rest of the year. The fare is $18, a dollar less for those over 62, and $14 for those who are 6-16. Reservations are required. Call (518) 523-4431.

The **Olympic Center** on Main Street is a multi-purpose facility that was used for the 1980 Olympics. It overlooks the speedskating oval where Eric Heiden won five gold medals. The center has four ice surfaces under one roof. It is used for hockey games, ice shows, public skating, etc. A self-guiding motor tour of the Olympic facilities takes about four hours and it is run daily 9 a.m. to 5 p.m. from late June until mid-October. Admission for the tour is $12, but $9 for senior citizens and ages 5-12. For non-tour use the center is open 9 a.m. to 5 p.m. with no admission charge.

Seven miles southeast on State Route 73 to Cascade Road the **Mount Van Hoevenberg Recreation Area** offers more than 30 miles of cross-country ski trails, luge and bobsled runs and a biathlon course. In summer, at the Nordic Lodge, films and a slide show are presented about sledding sports. Trolley rides and video-taped presentations are offered from mid-June until early October. Also available are tours of the bobsled and luge track areas and hiking trails. The Nordic Lodge rents ski equipment in season. A bobsled ride is offered Tuesday-Sunday from 1 p.m. to 3 p.m. if the weather permits.

The area is open daily from 9 a.m. to 4 p.m. Day-use charges are $3 while senior citizens and ages 6-12 are $2. These fees include special events. The cross-country ski area is $7, with senior citizens and those under 12 getting in for $6. A bobsled ride is $20, and a luge ride $10.

The **Olympic jumping complex** is located two miles southeast of Lake Placid on State Route 73. This is the training ski jump for the United States and Canadian Olympic teams. The **Kodak Sports Park** is a free-style skiing aerial training center. In summer, plastic matting simulates snow. There's a 295-foot tower with a glass-enclosed elevator that provides a majestic view of Mount Marcy. The complex is open daily from 9 a.m. to 5 p.m., mid-May to early October, and from 9 a.m. to 4 p.m. the rest of the year. Admission is $5, but reduced to $4 for senior citizens and ages 5-12. For further information call (518) 523-1655.

Where to Stay

Best Western-Golden Arrow Hotel is open all year. The one-person rate is $60-$138; two persons, $70-$138. There are some two-bedroom suites. A full range of indoor and outdoor sports is provided by the hotel and there is a restaurant. It is conveniently located in the center of Lake Placid. For reservations, write the hotel at 150 Main Street, 12946, or call (518) 523-3353.

The Holiday Inn-Grandview is in the center of the village on an elevated site that overlooks Mirror Lake. Most rooms have balconies. Bedroom units are also available. Room prices start at $46, ranging up to $186. There's an added fee for pets. Many indoor and outdoor sports are available. For reservations, write 1 Olympic Drive, Lake Placid, 12946, or call (518) 523-2556.

Howard Johnson's Resort Lodge is on Saranac Avenue, Route 86, and it is open all year. It has a lakeside location, and offers a senior discount. The rates range from $45 to $115. Indoor and outdoor activities are plentiful. Pets are accepted. There's an in-house restaurant. Write the hotel at 90 Saranac Avenue, 12946 for reservations or call (518) 523-9555.

The Lake Placid Hilton Resort is on Mirror Lake and offers a variety of rates depending upon the season. From 7/1-9/8 and 12/20-12/31 the rates range from $106 to $156. From 9/9-10/17, the rates are $96-$146. From 1/1-6/30 and 10/18-12/19, the rate is $56-$116. No pets are allowed. There's a full range of indoor/outdoor activities, with an in-house restaurant. For reservations, write the resort at 1 Mirror Drive, Lake Placid 12946, or call (518) 523-4411.

Lake Placid Village

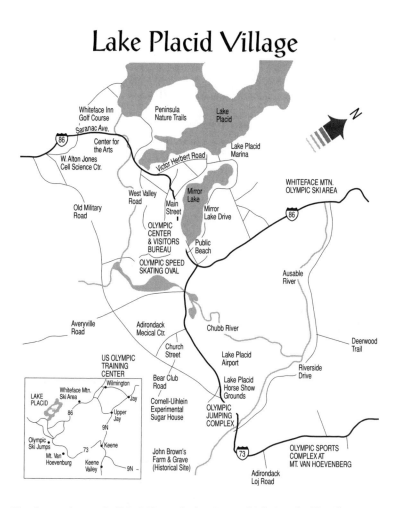

The best place of all is **Mirror Lake Inn** which is a half-mile west of the village and one block off State Route 86 on Mirror Lake Drive. No pets are permitted. There is a full line of indoor and outdoor activities, and a restaurant. From 6/25-9/5, 12/24-1/2, and 2/11-2/20 the rates are $94-$212. From 1/3-2/10, 2/21-3/21, 5/21-6/24 and 9/6-9/15 the rates are $86-$156. From 10/16-12/23 and 3/22-5/20 the rates are $74-$138. For reservations write the Inn at 5 Mirror Lake Drive, Lake Placid 12946, or call (518) 523-2544.

Where to Dine

Alpine Cellar Restaurant is three quarters of a mile east of the village on State Route 86, and just east of the traffic light at the junction with State Route 73. It serves mostly German food, but some Swiss is offered. It is open 5/15-10/31 and 12/21-3/29 from 5 p.m. to 10 p.m. For reservations call (518) 523-2180.

The Averil Conwell Dining Room is in the Mirror Lake Inn, and the restaurant overlooks the lake. It opens at 10 a.m. and 5:30 p.m. weekdays, and from 7:30 a.m.-11 a.m. and 5:30 p.m.-9 p.m. on Saturday and Sunday. It serves regional American food. For reservations call (518) 523-2544.

Lake Placid Manor serves continental food and it is located a mile and a quarter west of the village on State Route 86 to Whiteface Inn Road. Follow the signs. The restaurant is on the lake and it is open from 7:30 a.m. to 10 a.m. and 11:30 a.m. to 2:30 p.m. and from 6 p.m. to 9 p.m. Clothing restrictions apply. Casual attire is not permitted. It is closed from 4/1-4/30 and 11/1-11/30. For reservations call (518) 523-2573.

La Veranda is in the Holiday-Grandview and serves French and Italian entrees. It is open 6/1-9/15 from 6 p.m. to 9:30 p.m. but it is closed on Sunday. For reservations call (518) 523-3339.

Saranac Lake

Ten miles west of Lake Placid on Route 73 is Saranac Lake. It was first settled in 1819 and during the late 1800s and early 1900s it was a major tuberculosis treatment center. Today it is a popular vacation spot. The Alpo International dog sled races are held each year in late January, and a winter carnival takes place in mid-February. The latter features parades, an ice palace, ice sculptures, fireworks, and sporting events. In the summer the Can-Am Rugby Tournament is held in early August. Many cottages, inns and treatment centers still stand along Saranac Lake's winding streets. For further details call toll-free (800) 347-1992.

The **Charles Dickert Wildlife Museum** has a fine collection of stuffed animals that are native to the Adirondacks. It is in the library on Main Street and is open to the public Monday-Friday from 10 a.m. to 5 p.m., July 1-Labor Day. There is no admission charge.

Robert Louis Stevenson lived in Saranac Lake recovering from tuberculosis during the winter of 1887-1888. His cottage has been preserved with its original furniture. It is open Tuesday-Sunday from 9:30 a.m. until noon and 1 p.m.-4:30 p.m., July 1 to mid-September. There's a $1 admission charge for adults (50¢ for children under 16).

Where to Stay

Adirondack Comfort Inn offers a senior discount and is located three-quarters of a mile east of Saranac Lake on State Route 86. No pets. From 6/22-10/31 and 12/24-12/31, all rates are the same – $55-$115. These rates also apply from 11/1-12/23 and 4/1-6/21. For reservations write the Inn at 148 Lake Flower Avenue, Saranac Lake 12983, or call (518) 891-1970.

Burke's Lake Flower Motel, also with a senior discount, is three-quarters of a mile southeast of Saranac Lake. It is open all year and no pets are allowed. From 6/29-9/2, the rates for two persons, two beds are $55-$65. For the remaining months, the rate for two persons, two beds is $45-$55. For reservations write the motel at 15 Lake Flower Avenue 12983, or call (518) 891-2310.

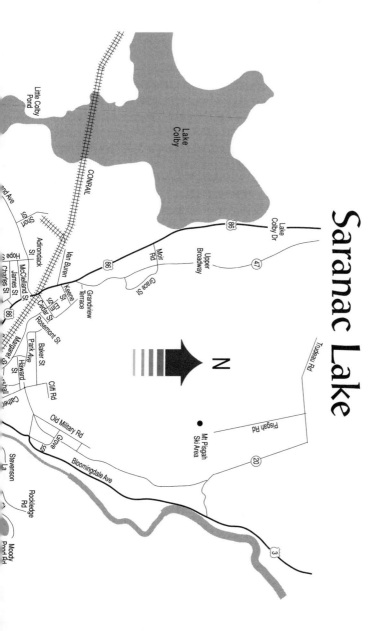

Lake Side Motel is three-quarters of a mile southeast of the village on State Route 86. It is open from 12/16-3/15 and 4/16-11/15. No pets. Rates range from $40-$75. For reservations, write the motel at 27 Lake Flower Avenue, 12983, or call (518) 891-4333.

Wilmington

You won't want to miss **Santa's Workshop at the North Pole**. It is located one-and-half miles west on State Route 431. There are craft shops, live entertainment, children's rides, storybook characters and, naturally, reindeer. Some activities are not always available. You can have breakfast with Santa Monday-Friday from 8:30 a.m. to 10 a.m. during July and August.

It is open daily 9:30 a.m.-5 p.m., July 1-Labor Day; Monday-Friday 10 a.m.-3 p.m. from the day after Labor Day to Columbus Day; Saturday and Sunday from 10 a.m. to 3:30 p.m. from the weekend before Thanksgiving to the weekend before December 25. Admission varies. Daily from July 1-Labor Day; Saturday and Sunday, the day after Labor Day-Columbus Day and the weekend before Thanksgiving weekend prior to December 25 the charges are $9.95; ages 3-17, $6.95; for those over 50, $4.95. For Saturday and Sunday, Memorial Day weekend-June 30, the admission is $2, and $1.50 for ages 3-17.

The **Whiteface Mountain Veterans' Memorial Highway** takes you close to the summit of the 4,867-foot Whiteface Mountain. This is a six-mile macadam road three-and-a-half miles west of Wilmington by State Route 341. There's adequate parking for your car and you can either climb the 1,000 feet to the summit or take an electric elevator in the summit's cone. Be prepared not only for a magnificent view across a hundred miles in any direction, including the St. Lawrence River and Lakes Champlain and Lake Placid. Be also prepared with sensible shoes for walking and warm clothing. Weather permitting, the road is open from 8 a.m. to 6 p.m., June 19-Labor Day; 9 a.m. to 4 p.m., May 21-June 18 and the day after

Labor Day to Columbus Day. Admission is $4 but senior citizens and ages 4-12 can get in for $3. Phone for details by calling (518) 523-1655 or 946-7175.

Three miles south of Wilmington on State Route 86 the **Whiteface Mountain Chairlift** offers a scenic ride to the summit of the 3,600-foot Little Whiteface Mountain. This is used in winter as the lift for a popular skiing resort. The lift operates daily 9 a.m. to 4 p.m., June 19-October 11 if the weather permits. Admission is $5, but those over 65 and under 13 can get in for $4. For details, call (800) 462-6236 toll-free.

Only a few miles away on route 86 between Wilmington and Lake Placid is one of the natural wonders of the world. **High Falls Gorge** was formed more than a billion years ago. The sparkling waters of the Ausable River rush over ancient granite rocks and seem to explode as they cascade 600 feet within a natural fissure carved through the ages by the effects of ice, water and wind. This is a camera paradise because of the easy access to the best views of the gorge. Modern bridges, paths and platforms permit you to get close to this phenomenal wonder. In addition, you'll see exotic wildflowers and ferns. The rock formations reveal strata that were carved before the existence of modern man. It is open from 8:30 a.m to 4:45 p.m. from Memorial Day to June 30, the day after Labor Day to Columbus Day from 9 a.m. to 4 p.m., and from July 1 to late August. Admission is $3.95, $3.15 if you are over 62, and $2 for ages 11-17 and $1.50 for ages 4-11. Call (518) 946-2278, or 946-2212 in winter.

Where to Stay & Dine

The Holiday Lodge is in the center of Wilmington on Route 86 and offers beautiful mountain views. From 3/1-12/24 and Friday-Saturday 12/25-2/26 the rates are $49.50-$79.50. Sunday-Thursday 12/25-2/28, the rates are $39.50-$79.50. Pets are allowed. Their restaurant is open from 7 a.m. to 11 p.m. and an hour later on

Friday and Saturday. For reservations, write the Lodge at P.O. Box 38, Wilmington 12997, or call (518) 946-2251.

The Hungry Trout Motor Inn is two miles west on Route 86 and the Ausable River. It is open from 12/1-4/1 and 5/1-11/1. From 6/8-11/1, the rates are $49-$59. From 12/1-4/1 and 5/1-6/7, the rates are $49-$79. The Inn's restaurant is open from 5/1-10/21 and 12/6-4/1 from 5 p.m. to 10 p.m. They accept pets. For reservations, write Hungry Trout Motor Inn, Wilmington, New York, 12997, or call (518) 946-2217.

Lodge Rock Motel faces Whiteface Mountain and is three miles southwest of Wilmington on State Route 86 and Placid Road. It is open all year. The rates range from $39-$93. For reservations write the Motel at HCR 2, Box 35, Wilmington 12997 or call (518) 946-2302.

North of Schroon Lake America's oldest western theme park, **Frontier Town**, holds rodeos, shootouts, stage and horse shows. Many actions that tamed the West are duplicated here from Memorial Day through Labor Day. From Memorial Day through June 22 it is open from 10 a.m. to 4:30 p.m. and thereafter from 9:30 a.m. to 5:30 p.m. Take Exit 29 off the Northway (I-87). For information call (518) 532-7181.

Ausable Chasm

This is a spectacular scenic wonder. It may be America's oldest tourist attraction, first having become popular in 1870. Every feature of the chasm can be explored as you proceed along stone galleries with stairs both up and down, and along steel bridges that cross the mighty gorge at various elevations. You'll see massive stone formations sculpted by nature into varied and majestic forms. The most famous is Elephant's Head rising above the river.

Your walk ends at Table Rock. Now you board a sturdy bateau for a thrilling ride down through the Grand Flume, where the water flows through towering cliffs only 20 feet apart. You pass the gigantic Sentry Box, then the Broken Needle, speeding through long rapids, around another deep basin, before descending into a second well-enclosed flume. After a final short ride through seething rapids you end up at the Chasm's lower end. A bus will be there to return you to the parking areas.

Ausable Chasm is open daily from 9 a.m. to 4 p.m., Memorial Day to Columbus Day. The fare is $11.95, but those over 55 and those with a military ID can get in for $9.95. Ages 6-11 are charged $7.95, and there's a family rate for up to five people of $38.95. There are discounts off the full rate for Memorial Day and Labor Day. The walking tour is $8.37, $6.95 for individuals over 55 and military, and ages 6-11 pay $5.57. Call (518) 834-7454 for further details.

There are no recommended places to stay or to dine near Ausable Chasm.

Tupper Lake

The **Big Tupper Lake Ski Area** off State Route 30 has slopes for all skiers. The resort has a municipal beach, park, campground, tennis courts, an 18-hole golf course and boat-launching sites. Call (518) 359-3328 for further details.

Where to Stay

Red Top Inn is three miles south of State Route 30 overlooking Big Tupper Lake. It is open all year, with rates of $38-$48. No pets. Apartments suitable for up to four persons are priced at $75-$80. For reservations, write the Inn at 90 Moody Road, HCR 1, 12986, or call (518) 359-9209.

Shaheen's Motel is three-quarters of a mile east of the village on State Routes 3 and 30. From 6/19-10/24, the single rate range is $41-$69; from 12/20-3/21, the rates range from $39-$69. From 3/22-6/18 the rates are $39-$55. No pets. For reservations write the motel at 310 Park Street, 12986, or call (518) 359-3384.

Tupper Lake Motel is half a mile east of the village on State Route 3 and 30. From 6/25-10/10, the rates range from $44 to $57. From 12/3-3/12 the rates are $37-$48. No pets. For reservations, write the motel at 259 Park Street, Tupper Lake, 12986 or call (518) 359-3381.

Blue Mountain Lake

The **Adirondack Museum** at Blue Mountain Lake, open daily from 9:30 a.m. to 5:30 p.m., Memorial Day weekend to October 15, has been called "the best of its kind in the world" by the *New York Times*. It portrays the history and culture of the Adirondacks through art, artifacts, exhibits and literature. It houses stage coaches and skillfully crafted guideboats in 22 exhibit buildings overlooking Blue Mountain Lake. Admission is $10 or $8.50 for those over 62, and $6 for ages 7-15. Call (518) 352-7311 for details.

There are no recommended places to stay or eat in the immediate area of Blue Mountain Lake.

Raquette Lake

Great Camp Sagamore, four miles from State Route 28, is a rustic summer retreat built in 1897 and expanded four years later. Typical of the 19th Century's great camps, the main lodge of logs and bark is beside Raquette Lake. There are quarters for caretakers, a bowling alley and a dining hall where food is available. A two-hour guided tour and a videotape presentation is available Thursday-

Tuesday at 10 a.m. and 1:30 p.m., August 25-October 13. Admission is $5 but those over 60 can get in for $2.50 and ages 5-12 are $2.50. For information, call (315) 354-4303, Ext. 5311.

There are no other recommended places to stay or eat in the vicinity.

Elizabethtown

One of the loveliest drives in the Adirondack region is U.S. 9. It extends through the Boquet River Valley to the south. At Elizabethtown, a block south of U.S. 9 and State Route 9N is the **Adirondack Center Museum and Colonial Garden** on Court Street. One of its shows depicts the history of the Champlain Valley. There are restored carriages, a mining exhibit, a doll collection, a formal garden and a nature trail. The museum is open Monday-Saturday from 9 a.m. to 5 p.m., Sunday from 1 p.m. to 5 p.m., mid-May to mid-October. The admission is $3.50 and a dollar cheaper for those over 60. Ages 6-18 can get in for $1.50. For information, call (518) 873-6466.

Where to Stay

The **Park Motor Inn** has a rate of $49.99 from 6/19 to 9/7. From 5/1-6/18, and 9/8-10/15, the rate for all categories is $42. From 10/16-4/30 the rate for all categories is $38.

There are no recommended places to eat in Elizabethtown.

Schroon Lake

Schroon Lake, in the heart of the Adirondack Park, offers four-season recreation and relaxation. It can be reached by taking I-87 and using Exit 27 from the south or Exit 28 from the north. It is only 90 minutes driving time north of Albany, and four-and-a-half hours from New York City. Boston is only four hours away. Lake Placid is 55 minutes from Schroon Lake and Lake George is a 25-minute drive. Schroon Lake Airport has no commercial service but small planes can land on its 3,000-foot runway.

Schroon Lake has all the ingredients for a winter holiday, with approximately 50 miles of free snowmobile trails that will take you through the mountains and over the lakes. The trails are well-marked and interconnecting. You can enjoy cross-country skiing on Schroon Lake or strike out on your own over surrounding wilderness trails. There's free ice-skating on the hockey rink or you can skate on the lake.

Ice fishing is particularly good here in the winter. Schroon Lake and Paradox Lake are exceptionally good fishing grounds. They both have landlocked salmon, small and large mouth bass, lake trout, great northern pike, pickerel and the usual run of small lake fish. There are quite a number of ponds in the area and most of them have trout. Four neighboring rivers and streams, Trout Brook, Minerva Stream, Hatch Pond Brook and the Schroon River, each have speckled, rainbow and brown trout, while Schroon River also has landlocked salmon and small mouth bass.

Where to Stay

The Red House on Sawmill Road is a mile east of Exit 28 off I-87, and four miles from Schroon Lake. It is situated on the banks of Paradox Brook at the junction of Sawmill Road and Route 74. Located on 150 acres of private land at the west end of Paradox Lake, its rooms with shared full bath and private guest parlor are $30 single occupancy and $50 double. Rental houses on the lake are also available. The facility offers swimming, tennis, fishing, canoeing, sailing and hiking trails. Write Helen Wildman, P.O. Box 125, Severeance, New York, 12872 or call (518) 532-7734. A bed and breakfast resort, it has been owned by the same family for five generations.

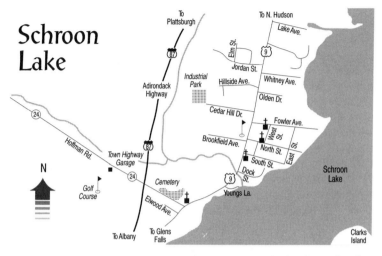

The Lake Paradox Club is located on 300 acres of private land at the west end of Paradox Lake in Adirondack Park. It is one mile east of Exit 28 on the Adirondack Northway (I-87) and just off Route 74. There are 11 rental houses here, with a private beach and docks. Most houses have four to six bedrooms, but usually with only one bathroom. They have electric kitchens and screened porches, and most have stone fireplaces. Some houses are available for rental any time of the year. They are completely furnished, except for linen and blankets. There is good fishing for bass, pike, lake trout and perch in Paradox Lake. During the winter there is good ice fishing and cross-country skiing. In the spring, canoeing and rafting are popular. Hiking is enjoyed the year around, but particularly during the fall color season. They rent 4-horsepower Mercury outboards. Boats on the lake are limited to 6 horsepower. Depending on the season and the size of the cottage, prices range from $400 a week, or $60 a day, to $700 a week. Electricity is separately metered for each house and during the busy season it is charged extra (about $25 a week). Firewood is billed at cost, usually $9 for one-eighth of a cord. The rentals are for six or fewer people in each house. For further information or reservations write: Helen Wildman, P.O. Box 125, Severance, New York, 12872, or call (518) 532-7734. There's an extra charge for more than six people, although children under three are free.

There are no recommended places to eat in Schroon Lake.

Lake George

Lake George Village is at the southern end of Lake George, which is 32 miles long. Ninety-two of its 365 islands have been developed for camping. At the village, there's a public beach and landings for steamboats and cruise boats. Speedboats, parasails and horse-drawn carriages are available nearby for rent.

Cruises on Lake George let youo truly appreciate the beauty of this region. The *Mohican*, owned by the Lake George Steamboat Company, has a narrated 4½-hour cruise around the lake and another cruise to Paradise Bay in half that time. The paddlewheeler *Minne-ha-ha* has hour-long shore cruises. Passengers may board or leave the *Minne-ha-ha* at Baldwin Landing in Ticonderoga for a one-way cruise on Lake George. The *Lac De Saint Sacrement* offers cruises for lunch and dinner, as well as moonlight cruises. From June 26-Labor Day, cruises depart daily at 9 a.m. Paradise Bay cruises leave daily at 2:30 p.m. From Memorial Day to Labor Day, May 10-15 and October 12-22, Paradise Bay cruises leave Monday-Friday at 11:30 a.m. The shoreline cruises leave daily at 10, noon, 1:30 p.m., 3 p.m., 4:30 p.m., 6 p.m. and 7:30 p.m., Memorial Day-June 25 and the day after Labor Day-Columbus Day. The luncheon cruise departs daily at 11:30 a.m. from May 15-Columbus Day, and also on May 9. The dinner cruises depart daily at 6:30 p.m. from June 26-Labor Day, and Sunday-Friday at 7 p.m. from September 9-October 15. Moonlight cruises leave Tuesday, Thursday and Saturday at 10 p.m. from July 3-August 28.

During the fall foliage season there are several scenic drives from Lake George that are incredibly beautiful. Take Exit 23 off I-87 and drive north on Route 9 through Warrensburg to the junction of

Routes 9 and 28. Then head northwest on Route 29, cross the Hudson River, and drive through Weverton and North Creek. You'll be driving along the Hudson River to North River. There are some outstanding overlooks to pause and enjoy the scenery. Proceed through Siamese Ponds Wilderness Region to Indian Lake, passing Lake Adirondack and Lake Abanake. Turn left at the sign to Sabael on Route 30. There's an overlook and rest area a few miles beyond that gives a spectacular view. The one-way trip from Lake George will take you approximately an hour and a quarter.

You might also try Route 9N from Lake George to Hague. Get off at Exit 22 from I-87 and take 9N north. You'll drive along the Lake George shoreline through Diamond Point and Bolton Landing. Turn right at the Bolton Library on Veterans Memorial Park Drive for a dockside view of the lake. Continue north on Route 9N over Tongue Mountain to Silver Bay. Be sure to stop at the overlook for another magnificent view. Continue north to Hague and stop at Town Park. The one-way trip will take only an hour.

Lake George has hundreds of pristine coves like this one, though many are crowded by camps in summer.

Hague can be reached by another road from Brant Lake on Route 8. Use Exit 25 from I-87 and go east of Route 8 to Brant Lake. Drive along the lake's shore and then continue on Route 8 through Pharaoh Wilderness and Dixon Forest. After you reach the hamlet of Graphite a short, curvy drive downhill brings you to the village of Hague. Turn right to Town Park and you'll have some outstanding views of Lake George. Retrace your route westward for more spectacular views of the Adirondack high peaks, or use Route 9N. This side trip takes an hour one-way.

Perhaps the best views of all are on the trip to Prospect Mountain on Veterans Memorial Highway. Take Exit 21 from I-87 and drive

a mile north on Route 9, turn left at the state highway entrance, and you'll get a 100-mile view from Prospect Mountain's 2,021-foot summit. A five-and-a-half mile, two-lane highway leads to the parking lot. Along this route you'll see beautiful views of Vermont's Green Mountains and New Hampshire's White Mountains. New York's high peaks will appear in all their glorious colors and, on a clear day, you'll even be able to see the Laurentian Mountains in Canada. Lake George Village is visible, with the Black Forest Range providing a backdrop. From the parking lot take the "viewmobile" to the summit for even more spectacular views including the remains of the world's largest cable railroad and the fireplace of what used to be the thriving Prospect Mountain Hotel. There are large picnic areas at the parking lot and at the summit. It is open daily from Memorial Day to October 18 from 9 a.m. to 6 p.m. It costs $5 for an automobile and $30 for a bus.

Prospect Mountain has a hiking trail that is one and five-eighths of a mile long leading to the summit. Red markers identify the trail. To reach the trail from Lake George Village turn west on Montcalm Street away from the lake to Smith Street. Turn south, one-half block, to a trailhead stop. The trail crosses I-87 on an elevated walkway. The climb to the summit is not difficult. It follows in part a road bed of an old funicular railway that once served a thriving summer hotel on the mountain.

Along "Million-Dollar-Half-A-Mile," factory outlets are available for shoppers, including Adirondack Factory, French Mountain Commons, Lake George Flags and Long Jam. They can be reached by going off I-87 at State Route 9, Exit 20.

In the town's center is **Fort William Henry Museum**. It is on U.S. 9. Built by the British in 1757 this replica of the original fort contains barracks, stockades and dungeons plus fort artifacts. The fort's history is told on an audiovisual program. The Living History tour, July through August, includes cannon firings and the molding of musket balls.

The fort is open from 9 a.m.-10 p.m. during July and August. From May-June and Labor Day-Columbus Day, it is open from 10 a.m. to 5 p.m. Admission is $6.40, but for those over 60 it is reduced to $5.35. For ages 6-11 the cost is $4.30. There is free parking in the rear. For further information, call (518) 668-5471.

Fort George, or what's left of it, is a half-mile south on U.S. 9 in **Lake George Battlefield Park**. It includes an Indian monument and a memorial to Jesuit missionary Father Jogues. It is open daily from 9 a.m. to 8 p.m., mid-June through Labor Day. From early May to mid-June it is open on Saturday and Sunday from 9 a.m. to 8 p.m. It costs $3 to park your vehicle and picnicking is permitted. For details about the park call (518) 668-3352.

Where to Stay

The **Admiral Motel** is in the town's center and is open 5/1-10/25, with varying seasonal rates. From 6/28-9/7 the rate is $65 for two persons and one bed, or $75-$85 for two persons and two beds. The rest of the season the rate is $42 for two persons, one bed. For two persons and two beds, it ranges from $48-$52. No pets. For reservations, write 437 Canada Street, Lake George 12845, or call (518) 668-2097.

The **Balmoral Motel** is at the junction of U.S. 9 and 9N. From 6/20-9/7 the rates are $52-$98. From 9/8-6/19 the rates are $30-$72. No pets. For reservations, write 444 Canada Street, 12845, or call (518) 668-2673.

Best Western of Lake George has seasonal rates. From 6/25-9/5 the rates are $95-$125. From 5/1-6/24 and 9/6-10/10, they are $65-$95. From 10/11-4/30, rates are $45-$55.

Dunham's Bay Lodge is five miles northeast on State Route 9L. It is open 5/21-10/11. From 6/25-9/7 the rates are $115-$140. From 5/21-6/24 the rates are $75-$85. Some housekeeping units are available. For reservations call (518) 793-3196, or write the Lodge at RR 1, Box 1179, 12845.

French Mountain Motel is four and a quarter miles south on U.S. 9 and a quarter-mile south of the junction with State Route 79. From 7/24-9/6 the rates are $84; from 6/19-7/23, $68; and from 9/7-6/18, $48. For reservations, write the motel at P.O. Box 3094, 12845, or call (518) 792-5904.

The Georgian is a quarter-mile north of Lake George on U.S. 9 and State Route 9N, one half-mile southeast of I-87's Exit 22 on the lakefront. From 9/7-6/24 the rate is $55-$125. There is a dining room. No pets. For reservations, write 384 Canada Street, 12845 or call (518) 668-5401.

Holiday Inn Turf at Lake George offers a senior discount. It is located three-quarters of a mile south of Lake George on U.S. 9 and State Route 9N, three-quarters of a mile north of I-87's Exit 21. It is open 4/30-10/18. From 6/30-9/7 rates are $115-$210. From 6/1-6/29, rates are $60-$135. From 9/8-5/31 rates are $65-$125. No pets. For reservations, write the Inn at Route 9, Box 231, 12845, or call (518) 668-5781.

The Mohican Hotel is three and a half miles south of Lake George on U.S. 9 and one-half mile north of I-87's Exit 22. From 6/26-9/5 rates range from $49-$140. From 9/6 to 6/25 rates range from $48-$78. There also are some two-bedroom suites at $135-$180 in-season and $88-$130 off-season. No pets. For reservations write R.R. 3, Box 3335, 12845, or call (518) 792-0474.

The Quarters at Fours Seasons Inn is one mile south on State Route 9N, and a quarter-mile north of I-87's Exit 22 on Lake Shore Drive. An apartment motel, it has 25 units. From 5/26 to 9/4 they charge $1,250-$1,800 weekly for two persons with two beds. From 9/1-6/17 the weekly rent drops to $700-$950. No pets. For reservations, write RD 2, Box 2367, 12845, or call (518) 668-4901.

Roaring Brook Ranch and Tennis Resort is two and a half miles south of Lake George on State Route 9N, one mile west of I-87's Exit 21. From 6/30-9/3 the rate for two persons with two beds is $154-$164; from 9/4-10/12 and 5/15-6/29 the rate for two people, two beds, is $134-$144. No pets. For reservations write Lake George 3, 12845, or call (518) 668-5767.

Where to Dine

Bayberry Corners Restaurant is on State Route 149, two and a half miles east of its junction with State Route 9. Make a right on 149 and Bay Road. The restaurant opens at 11 a.m. and serves American food. It is closed on Mondays, as well as 11/25 and 12/25. For reservations call (518) 798-6492.

The East Cove Restaurant serves American food in a log cabin atmosphere, and it has a Sunday buffet. It is three-quarters of a mile east on U.S. 9L. The restaurant is closed 11/21-11/28. Call for reservations (518) 668-5265.

The Log Jam is four and a half miles south of Lake George at the junction of U.S. 9 and State Route 149. It has a log cabin atmosphere, serves American food, and is open for lunch and dinner. For reservations call (518) 798-1155.

Marlo's Restaurant is a quarter-mile north of Lake George on U.S. 9 and SR-9N, one quarter-mile south of I-87's Exit 22 at 469 Canada Street. It serves Italian food. For reservations call (518) 668-2665.

The Market Grille serves American food and is a quarter-mile north of Lake George Village on U.S. 9 and State Route 149. It is open from 7 a.m. to 10 p.m. Call (518) 745-8152.

Montcalm Restaurant serves American food and is located four and a half miles south of Lake George on U.S. 9 at I-87's Exit 20. It offers a senior discount. It is open weekdays at 5 p.m. and Sundays at noon. For reservations call (518) 793-6601.

Shoreline Restaurant serves American food. It is on the lake at the foot of Kurosaka Lane. It is normally open from 8 a.m. to 11 p.m. For reservations call (518) 668-2875.

Trolley Steak and Seafood is on Canada Street where U.S. 9 and State Route 9N meet and a mile from I-87's Exit 21. It is open most of the year for dinner. For reservations call (518) 668-2875.

Sutton's Farm Market, eight miles south of Lake George on Route 9 is highly honored for its breakfasts and lunches. It is open Friday nights for dinner between 5 and 9 p.m. Modest prices for superb food.

Saratoga Springs

Saratoga Springs, a small city of 25,000 people, is unique in the Adirondack region. Visually, it is a delight and during the summer months the nightlife is unsurpassed for the area. Known since Indian times for the reputed medicinal qualities of its spring waters, it has become a year-round playground. Lovely Victorian-style homes are scattered throughout the city. They were built by wealthy racing fans.

Harness racing draws large crowds from mid-April until mid-November. **The Saratoga Harness Racing Track** is located off Nelson Avenue. For details, call (518) 584-2110. In August, spectators can watch thoroughbred races at Saratoga Race Course on Union Avenue. For details, call (518) 584-6200. If you want to bring children to the races, it is suggested you call in advance to find out about any restrictions. Admittance to pari-mutuel betting facilities varies in New York State.

There are many alpine and cross-country skiing facilities in Saratoga Springs, along with ice skating and snow-shoeing trails.

The Urban Cultural Park Visitor Center is open from spring through fall across from Congress Park. For information call (518) 587-3241. Summer guided tours are conducted by City Tours, leaving the visitor center and major hotels. Mike's Guided Tours offers two-and-a-half hour tours including stops at the Historical

Saratoga County

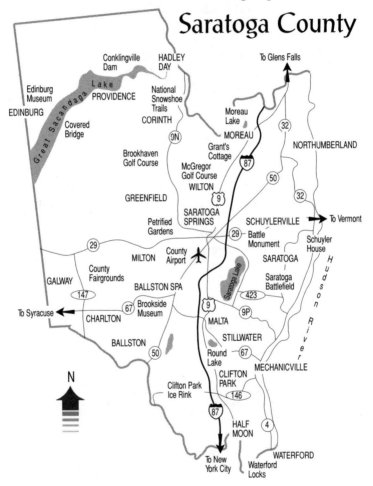

Society of Saratoga Springs Museum and at Yaddo. The latter is a quarter-mile west of I-87's Exit 14 on Union Avenue. This is an incredibly beautiful private estate made available for visual artists, writers, poets and composers to work in a relaxing environment. The rose gardens are open to the public from dawn to dusk. For Mike's Tours, call (518) 885-2650.

The Saratoga Spa State Park, which includes the Saratoga Performing Arts Center and the August home of the Philadelphia Orchestra, is north of I-87 at Exit 13N. The Spa Summer Theater offers performances from October through April. There are bath houses, mineral springs, walking trails, golf courses and picnic pavilions. It is open from 8 a.m. to dusk and there is no admission charge. There is a $3 parking fee from Memorial Day to Labor Day but none at other times. For program and ticket information call (518) 584-2535 or 587-3330.

The Saratoga National Historical Park is eight miles south of Schuylerville on U.S. 4 and encompasses 2,800 acres. It lies along the west side of the Hudson River in partially wooded country. The park was created in memory of those who fought in the Battle of Saratoga on September 19-October 7, 1777, defeating General John Burgoyne's British army.

Burgoyne surrendered on October 17 near Schuylerville, or old Saratoga, to General Horatio Gates' army. The British had tried to split the colonial army by driving from Canada to Albany, while another British force came up from New York City. This "turning point" of the American Revolution made it possible for General George Washington's army to survive and eventually beat the British. The Saratoga Monument, eight miles from the battlefield, commemorates Burgoyne's surrender.

Benedict Arnold, who later turned traitor, helped to secure victory for the Americans, although he had no command responsibility. At Breymann's Redoubt he galloped through cross-fire to rally the American troops and secure victory. He was wounded for the second time in this war (the first was at Quebec) and in the same leg. Despite his later treachery in offering to turn over West Point to the British, his heroic charge at Saratoga is recalled by a statue of a granite boot with epaulets, and an inscription describing Arnold's service to his country, but without mentioning his name.

Fraser Hill, the highest point in the park, has a visitor's center that provides a view of the battlefield and the surrounding area. There are daily theater programs and picnics are permitted.

You can drive around the park on a nine-mile road. There are 10 stops to indicate important sites. There's a $3 vehicle fee for this trip but hiking and biking trails cost only $1 per person. The trails are free for the driving tour. The park is open from 9 a.m. to 5:30 p.m. daily during July and August and from 9 a.m. to 5 p.m. the rest of the year. It is closed on January 1, Thanksgiving and December 25. For further information call (518) 664-9821.

Brochures and maps of Saratoga Springs are available from the Saratoga County Chamber of Commerce, 494 Broadway, Saratoga Springs, NY 12866. Their phone number is (518) 584-3255.

There's an 1870s casino off Broadway on U.S. 9 in Congress Park. It has Italian sculpture gardens where well-known sculptors, including Daniel Chester French, are represented. He created the seated Lincoln in the Washington, D.C. Lincoln Memorial. At the **Historical Society of Saratoga Springs Museum** you can trace the growth of the city from a rural village to its present status as a world-renowned resort.

The Casino and Congress Park are open Monday-Tuesday, and Thursday-Saturday from 10 a.m. to 4 p.m.; Wednesday and Sunday from 1 p.m. to 4 p.m. during June-October. From February-May and November and December, they are open Wednesday-Sunday from 1 p.m. to 4 p.m. Admission is $2. Students and senior citizens with ID can enter for $1.50. Children under 7 are admitted free. For information, call (518) 584-6920.

The National Museum of Dance, on U.S. 9 (take Broadway one mile south) has interesting dance exhibits including a Dance Hall of Fame. Guided tours are given on Sunday at 1 p.m. The museum is open Tuesday-Sunday, 10 a.m.-6 p.m. from July 1-Labor Day; Saturday and Sunday from 10 a.m. to 6 p.m. on Memorial Day weekend-June 30. Admission is $3, but for those over 62 and students from 13-21 the charge is $2. Call (518) 584-2225.

The National Museum of Racing and Hall of Fame has exhibits on the past, present and future of Thoroughbred Racing in America, including paintings and sculptures. It is located at Union Avenue and Ludlow Street. The Hall of Fame honors horses, jockeys and trainers. Through videotapes and a skeleton horse, selective breeding is described. Videotapes also have well-known trainers and jockeys to explain training and racing techniques. It is open daily from 9 a.m. to 5 p.m. in August; Monday-Saturday from 10 a.m. to 4:30 p.m. and at noon on Sunday the rest of the year. It is closed on major holidays except for July 4. Admission is $3 but those over 65 and ages 5-16 are admitted for $2. For further information call (518) 584-1400.

Where to Stay

The Adelphi Hotel is on Broadway in the center of the city. It is an historic country inn. Pets are allowed. From 5/28 to 8/30 the rates ($130-$290) are the same for one or two persons. From 7/1-7/27 the rates are $80-$175. From 5/1-6/30, and 9/1-10/31, the rates are $70-$150. For reservations, write the hotel at 365 Broadway, Saratoga Springs, N.Y. 12866, or call (518) 587-4688.

The Gideon-Putnam Hotel is a mile west of the city on U.S. 9 in Saratoga Spa State Park. With sumptuous public rooms and a conservative atmosphere, it was built in 1930 as a Georgian-style hotel. From 7/28-8/30, single and double rooms are all priced at $246. From 5/1-7/27 and 9/1-10/31, the single rate is $100, or $119 for a double room with one or two beds. From 11/1-4/30, the single rate is $77, or $93 for a double room with one or two beds.

There is a dining room in the hotel with à la carte entrées ranging from $17-$20. For reservations, write the hotel at P.O. Box 476, Saratoga Springs, 12866, or call (518) 584-3000.

The Holiday Inn is one block south on U.S. 9 at the junction of State Route 50. It offers a senior discount. From 7/28-8/29 the single or double rate is $189. From 6/18-7/27 and 8/30-9/5 the single rate is $76 and the double rate is $86. From 4/30-6/17 and 9/6-10/30 the single rate is $65 and the double rate is $75. There's an in-house dining room and pets are permitted. For reservations write the Inn at Broadway and Circular Street, 12866, or call (518) 584-4550.

The Inn at Saratoga is a Clarion Carriage House Inn. It is located on the west side of Saratoga Springs at the junction of Highways 50 and 9. From 7/29-8/31 the rate is $210-$245. From 6/21-7/28 the rate is $115-$135. From 4/26-6/20 and 9/1-11/1 the rate is $95-$115. Pets are allowed. A continental breakfast is served. For reservations write the Inn at 231 Broadway, 12866, or call (518) 583-1890.

The Ramada Renaissance Hotel is downtown on State Route 50. From I-87 take Exit 15. From 7/29-8/31, the rate is $145-$235. From 5/1-7/26 and 9/1-11/14, the rate is $76-$98. From 11/15-4/30, the rate is $72-$92. No pets. For reservations write the hotel at 534 Broadway, 12866, or call (518) 584-7430.

Where to Dine

The Canterbury, serving continental food, is four miles southeast of the city on State Route 9P. From I-87 use Exit 14 and drive one and a quarter-mile on State Route 9P to 500 Union Avenue. It is open from 5:30 p.m.-10 p.m., or Sunday from 2 p.m. to 9 p.m. For reservations, call (518) 587-9653.

Professor Moriarty's Dining and Drinking Salon is at 432 Broadway in the town's center. It serves American food from 11:30

a.m.-10 p.m. From 7/17-8/31 it is only open from 9 a.m until noon. For reservations call (518) 587-5981.

Spring Water Inn is at the corner of Union Avenue and Nelson, opposite the thoroughbred racetrack. From I-87 take Exit 14 and drive two miles west on Union Avenue to number 139. It is open from 5 p.m. to 10 p.m. The Inn is closed on Monday except from 7/1-8/25 and 12/23-12/31. For reservations call (518) 584-6440.

Public Campsites

The New York State Department of Environmental Conservation provides many fine campsites in the Adirondacks. They allow six people for each campsite. Unlike private campsites, they do not have electrical hookups. The state charges $9 to $15 per night. Each site provides the following, except as noted: Trailer and/or tent sites, picnicking, trailer dumping station, showers, boat and canoe rental, boat launching facilities, swimming, bath houses, lifeguards, fishing, hiking. They are usually on a pond or lake, river or stream, and power boats are allowed.

1. Alger Island, off Route 28, South Shore Road, eight miles east of Old Forge (315) 369-3224. Access by boat only. No trailer dumping station, no showers, no river or stream, no boat or canoe rental, no hiking.

2. Ausable Point, Route 9, 12 miles south of Plattsburgh, (518) 561-7080. No boat or canoe rentals, no hiking.

3. Brown Tract Pond, Route 28, seven miles east of Eagle Bay. (315) 354-4412. No showers, river or stream available. No powerboats.

4. Buck Pond, off Route 86, and six miles north of Gabriels. (518) 891-3449.

New York State

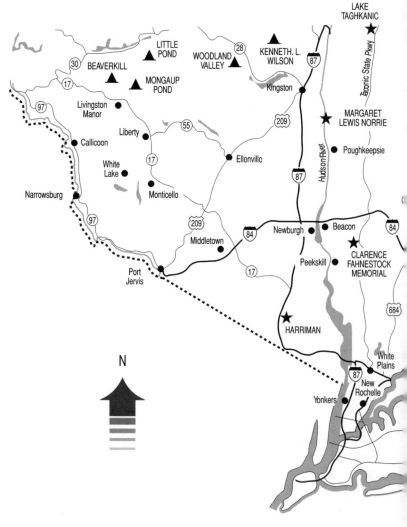

LAKE
TAGHKANIC

LITTLE
POND

BEAVERKILL

WOODLAND
VALLEY

28

KENNETH. L.
WILSON

87

MONGAUP
POND

Kingston

Taconic State Pkwy

30

17

97

Livingston
Manor

Liberty

55

209

MARGARET
LEWIS NORRIE

Poughkeepsie

Callicoon

White
Lake

17

Ellonvillc

87

Hudson River

Narrowsburg

Monticello

97

209

84

Newburgh

Beacon

84

Middletown

Peekskill

CLARENCE
FAHNESTOCK
MEMORIAL

Port
Jervis

17

684

HARRIMAN

White
Plains

87

New
Rochelle

Yonkers

N

ampsites

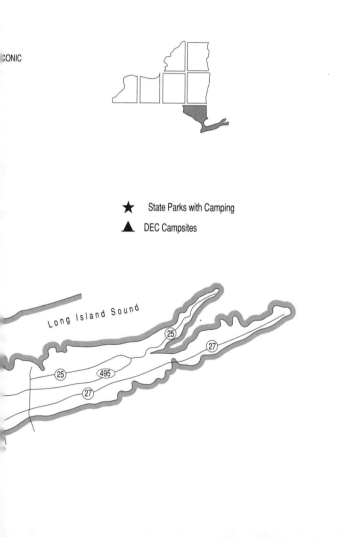

New York State Campsites

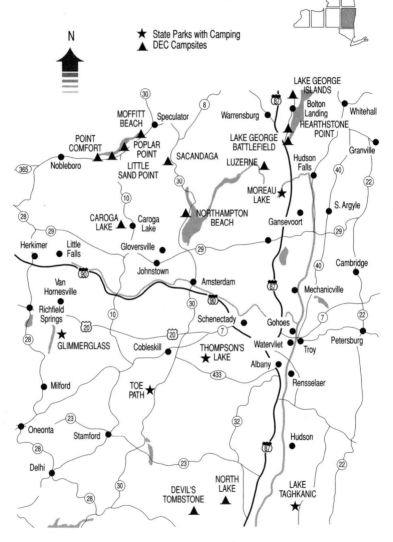

★ State Parks with Camping
▲ DEC Campsites

N

LAKE GEORGE ISLANDS
Bolton Landing
Whitehall
HEARTHSTONE POINT
Warrensburg
LAKE GEORGE BATTLEFIELD
Granville
MOFFITT BEACH
Speculator
POPLAR POINT
LUZERNE
Hudson Falls
POINT COMFORT
SACANDAGA
Nobleboro
LITTLE SAND POINT
MOREAU LAKE
S. Argyle
CAROGA LAKE
Caroga Lake
NORTHAMPTON BEACH
Gansevoort
Herkimer
Little Falls
Gloversville
Cambridge
Van Hornesville
Johnstown
Amsterdam
Mechanicville
Richfield Springs
Schenectady
Gohoes
GLIMMERGLASS
Cobleskill
THOMPSON'S LAKE
Watervliet
Troy
Petersburg
Milford
TOE PATH
Albany
Rensselaer
Oneonta
Stamford
Hudson
Delhi
DEVIL'S TOMBSTONE
NORTH LAKE
LAKE TAGHKANIC

New York State Campsites

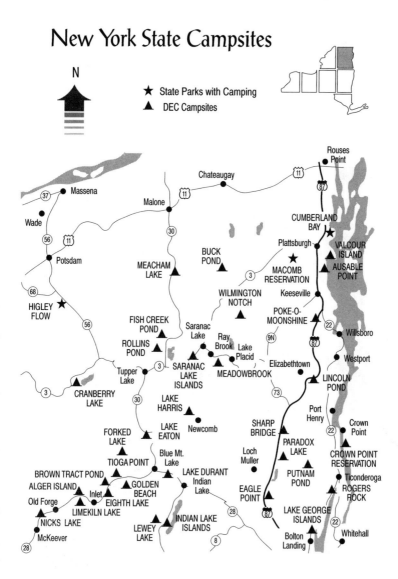

N

★ State Parks with Camping
▲ DEC Campsites

Rouses Point

Chateaugay

Massena

Malone

Wade

Potsdam

CUMBERLAND BAY

Plattsburgh

VALCOUR ISLAND

BUCK POND

MEACHAM LAKE

MACOMB RESERVATION

AUSABLE POINT

Keeseville

WILMINGTON NOTCH

HIGLEY FLOW

POKE-O-MOONSHINE

FISH CREEK POND

Saranac Lake

Willsboro

ROLLINS POND

Ray Brook

Lake Placid

Westport

Tupper Lake

SARANAC LAKE ISLANDS

MEADOWBROOK

Elizabethtown

LINCOLN POND

CRANBERRY LAKE

LAKE HARRIS

Port Henry

Crown Point

LAKE EATON

Newcomb

SHARP BRIDGE

FORKED LAKE

Blue Mt. Lake

Loch Muller

PARADOX LAKE

CROWN POINT RESERVATION

TIOGA POINT

LAKE DURANT

BROWN TRACT POND

GOLDEN BEACH

Indian Lake

PUTNAM POND

Ticonderoga

ALGER ISLAND

EIGHTH LAKE

EAGLE POINT

ROGERS ROCK

Old Forge

Inlet

LIMEKILN LAKE

NICKS LAKE

INDIAN LAKE ISLANDS

LAKE GEORGE ISLANDS

McKeever

LEWEY LAKE

Bolton Landing

Whitehall

New York State Campsites

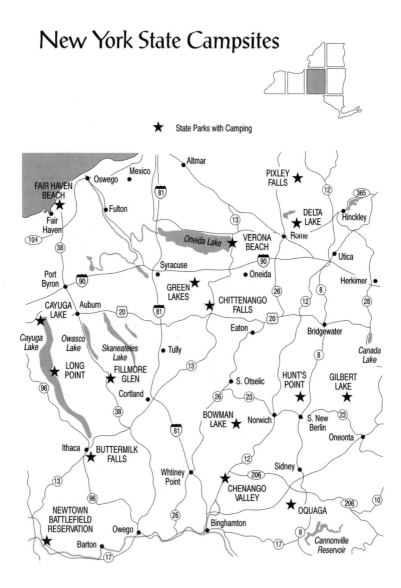

★   State Parks with Camping

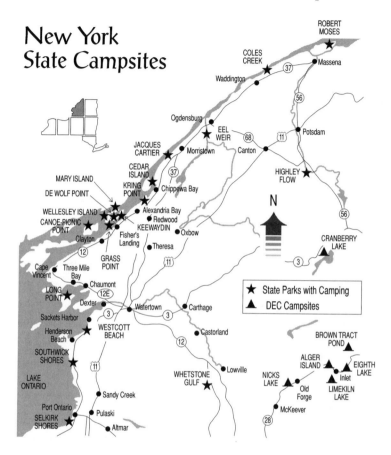

New York State Campsites

★ State Parks with Camping

▲ DEC Campsites

5. Caroga Lake, Route 29A, nine miles north of Gloversville. (518) 835-4241. No river or stream, no boat or canoe rentals.

6. Cranberry Lake, off Route 3, and 1.5 miles south of Cranberry Lake Village. (315) 848-2315. No river or stream, no boat or canoe rentals.

7. Crown Point Reservation, off Route 9N, and eight miles north of Crown Point. (518) 597-3603. No river or stream, no boat or canoe rentals, no swimming, no hiking.

8. Eagle Point, U.S. Route 9, and two miles north of Pottersville. (518) 494-2220. No river or stream, no boat or canoe rentals, no hiking.

9. Eighth Lake, Route 28, two miles north of Pottersville. (315) 354-4120. No river or stream.

10. Fish Creek Pond, Route 30, 12 miles north of Tupper Lake. (518) 891-4560.

11. Forked Lake, off Route 30, and three miles west of Deerland Village. (518) 624-6646. No trailer dumping station, no showers, no river or stream, no swimming.

12. Golden Beach, Route 28, three miles east of Raquette Lake. (315) 354-4230. No river or stream.

13. Hearthstone Point, Route 9N, two miles north of Lake George Village. (518) 668-5193. No picnicking, no river or stream, no boat rentals or boat launching facilities, no bath houses.

14. Indian Lake Islands, Route 30, 14 miles north of Speculator. (518) 648-5300. Access by boat only. No trailer and/or tent sites, no trailer dumping station, no showers, no rivers or streams, no swimming.

15. Lake Durant, Route 28, three miles south of Blue Mountain Lake. (518) 352-7797. No river or stream.

16. Lake Eaton, Route 30, two miles west of Long Lake. (518) 624-2641. No river or stream.

17. Lake George Battleground, U.S. Route 9, a quarter-mile south of Lake George Village. (518) 668-3348. No picnicking, no pond or lake, no river or stream, power boats not allowed, no swimming, fishing or hiking.

18. Lake George Islands, Bolton Landing, (518) 644-9696. No trailer dumping station, no showers, no river or stream, no power-boats, no swimming.

19. Lake Harris, off Route 28N, three miles north of Newcomb. (518) 582-2503. No river or stream.

20. Dewey Lake, Route 30, 14 miles north of Speculator. (518) 648-5266. No river or stream.

21. Limekiln Lake, off Route 28, three miles southeast of Inlet. (315) 357-4401. No river or stream.

22. Lincoln Pond, six miles south of Elizabethtown on County Route 7. (518) 942-5292. No river or stream, no boat launching, no hiking.

23. Little Sand Point, off Route 8, three miles west of Piseco. (518) 548-7585. No picnicking, no showers, no river or stream and no bath houses.

24. Luzerne, Route 9N, eight miles southwest of Lake George Village. (518) 696-2031. No river or stream, no hiking.

25. Meacham Lake, Route 30, 19 miles north of Lake Clear Junction. (518) 483-5116. No river or stream, no hiking.

26. Moffitt Beach, Route 8, four miles west of Speculator. (518) 548-7102. No river or stream.

27. Nick's Lake, off Route 29, 1.5 miles southwest of Old Forge. (315) 369-3314. No river or stream.

28. Northampton Beach, Route 30, 1.5 miles south of Northville. (518) 863-6000. No river or stream.

29. Paradox Lake, Route 74, two miles east of Severance. (518) 532-7451. No river or stream.

30. Point Comfort, off Route 8, four miles west of Piseco. (518) 548-7586. No showers and no river or stream.

31. Poke-O-Moonshine, U.S. Route 9, six miles south of Keeseville. (518) 834-9045. No trailer dumping station, no pond or lake, river or stream, no hiking.

32. Poplar Point, off Route 8, two miles west of Piseco. (518) 548-8031. No showers and no river or stream.

33. Putnam Pond, off Route 74, six miles west of Ticonderoga. (518) 585-7280. No boat or canoe rentals.

34. Rogers Rock, Route 9N, three miles north of Hague. (518) 585-6746. No river or stream, no rowboats/canoes and no fishing.

35. Sacandaga, Route 30, four miles south of Wells. (518) 924-4121. No river or stream, no power boats allowed, no rowboats/canoes, no swimming.

36. Saranac Lake Islands, off Route 3, and five miles west of the village of Saranac Lake. (518) 891-3170. No trailer dumping station, no showers, no river or stream, no swimming, no bath houses or lifeguards.

37. Sharp Bridge, U.S. Route 9, 15 miles north of Schroon Lake. (518) 532-7538. No pond or lake, no boats, no swimming, lifeguards or bath houses.

38. Taylor Pond, Silover Lake Road, nine miles northwest of Ausable Forks. No picnicking, showers or river or stream, no swimming, bath houses or lifeguards.

39. Tioga Point, Raquette Lake, (518) 354-4230. No trailer and/or tent sites, no trailer dumping station, no showers, no river or stream, no boat launching or swimming.

40. Wilmington Notch, Route 86, 3.5 miles west of Wilmington. (518) 946-7172. No pond or lake, no power boats allowed, no rowboats or canoes.

The *Empire Passport* provides unlimited free vehicle entry to most state parks and recreation areas during the calendar year January 1-December 31. The pass does not cover activity fees. Purchase may be made in person at most state parks or recreation centers, or by mail from State Parks, Albany, New York, 12238.

The *Access Pass* is available to New Yorkers with qualifying disabilities. It provides free entry and use of state park and recreation areas and their facilities, except those services and facilities that are operated by concessionaires. Application forms are available from State Parks, Albany, New York, 12238.

New camping and cabin reservation regulations went into effect in 1990 for all New York State Parks. The reservation phone number is (800) 456-CAMP. Some parks will grant specific sites upon request.

Senior citizens who are New York State residents and 62 years of age or older can have unlimited weekday and non-holiday access to all state parks and receive discounts on certain fees. A driver's license or other proof of age must be shown.

Hiking Trails

The High Trails

Mt. Marcy, or Tahawus as the Indians called it, was first climbed by white men in 1837. Professor Emmons and his party had to struggle through virgin forest which, especially in the dense alpine growth of pure scrubby balsam near the top of the mountain, made it difficult to reach the summit. Today there are four well-marked trails which converge at or near the mountain's peak.

Tahawus, or the Cloud Splitter of the Indians, was renamed Mt. Marcy after Governor Marcy. It is the highest peak in the Adirondacks and in the state, rising to 5,344 feet above sea level. It is surrounded by the other high peaks of the MacIntyre Range, which extends in a southwesterly and northeasterly direction through the west-central portion of Essex County. The divide between the Hudson and the St. Lawrence Rivers passes over the summit and, to the southwest, at the base of the cone lies Lake Tear-of-the-Clouds – the highest lake source of the Hudson River.

From the north the Van Hoevenberg Trail, seven miles in length, is the shortest trail to the mountain. It begins at the automobile parking lot of Adirondack Loj, which is nine miles by highway from Lake Placid Village.

An alternate route to Marcy is available. This seven-mile trail begins at an open parking area on state land at South Meadows. The walk is approximately three miles to Marcy Dam along the yellow marked fire truck trail.

Marcy may also be reached from the north through Avalanche Pass, by way of the Van Hoevenberg Trail and Lakes Avalanche and Colden. From Lake Colden the trail follows the Opalescent and Feldspar Brooks, past Lake Tear-of-the-Clouds, to the peak.

The third trail is via Indian Pass. Starting on the right side of the road to Adirondack Loj just before the lodge is reached, this trail leads over a low divide to a branch of the Ausable River, then up to Indian Pass, which lies between Mt. Marshall and the appropriately named Wallface Mountain, with its vertical face of 1,000 feet. From the pass, Santanoni Mountain may be seen directly ahead. After descending Indian Pass Brook about three miles, the trail passes over the end of the McIntyre Range to Calamity Brook, following it up past Calamity Pond and the monument erected to David Henderson, who accidentally shot himself while hunting nearby, to the Flowed Lands and Lake Colden, where it joins the trail from Avalanche Pass. The total distance is 17.15 miles.

The trail to Scott and Wallface Ponds leaves the Indian Pass Trail just east of Scott's Clearing, crossing the brook about 25 feet east of the dam, and proceeds along the southwest shore of the pond in a northwesterly direction to Wallace Ponds, a distance of seven miles. The total distance from Indian Pass Trail to Wallace Ponds is 2.25 miles.

Of the eastern approaches from Keene Valley, the Johns Brook Trail, via Silent Rock, is the oldest and best known trail. It begins at the main corners in Keene Valley Lodge and follows up Johns Brook past Bushnell Falls and the natural rock shelter known as Silent Rock Camp. The distance from Keene Valley to the top of Marcy is 9.95 miles, and the ascent is 4,250 feet. This is the trail that my cousin Frank Morrison and I took to Marcy in the early 1930s.

Today an Interior Department headquarters is maintained by the Department of Environmental Conservation on the trail and is located 4.6 miles from Keene Valley.

The Hopkins Trail from Johns Brook to Marcy through the notch south of Tabletop Mountain from Keene Valley Village follows the Slant Rock Trail to a point just beyond Bushnell Falls where it branches, keeping on the north side of Johns Brook, to an intersection with the Van Hoevenberg Trail on the top of Plateau. The distance to Marcy over this trail is 10.5 miles. This is a difficult trip to make in one day.

The Range Trail is the most scenic as well as the most difficult. It begins at Keene Valley and follows up the Johns Brook Trail to Orebed Brook, then to the saddle between Saddleback and Gothic Mountains and over the summit of Saddleback and Basin mountains to the Slant Rock Trail. The trail is very steep in places, especially on the west side of Saddleback and both sides of Basin. The distance over this trail to Marcy is 11.75 miles.

In the south, the approaches to Marcy are from Tahawus via Calamity Brook, Flowed Lands and Lake Colden. Through the courtesy of the National Lead Company, public access is now available to the Lake Colden, Mt. Marcy, Indian Pass and Cold River sections from the south through what was formerly the Tahawus Club. This route is 11.55 miles.

Another southern approach takes you from Tahawus via Lake Sally, the East River, Hanging Spear Falls, the Flowed Lands and Lake Colden. The trailhead is located on the Tahawus Road. Travel east from Newcomb Village on State Highway 28N to where it intersects with the Blue Ridge Road. Follow the Blue Ridge Road 1.5 miles to where it intersects with the Tahawus Road. Turning left, follow the Tahawus Road 8.21 miles to a parking lot on the right. The trail starts at the parking lot. From this point, follow yellow markers passing Lake Jimmy and Lake Sally. The trail reaches the East River, which it follows in a northerly direction. The trail crosses the East River on a suspension foot bridge. Continue on yellow markers to the Twin Brook lean-to. Follow red markers across the stream. The trail then follows up the Opalescent River, past Hanging Spear Falls, to the dam forming the Flowed Lands and around the west and north sides of this body of water to Lake Colden. The total distance to Marcy over this route from the trailhead is 12 miles and the ascent 3,600 feet.

The trail from Elk Lake is one of the oldest. It is marked with blue markers and starts a half-mile south of Elk Lake on the west side of the road. The highway to Elk Lake is public as far as the Clear Pond Gate, but traffic may proceed to the parking lot a half-mile south of Elk Lake when the road is not posted.

The trail to Boreas Mountain begins at the Clear Pond Gate. Both the trail to Boreas Mountain and to Mt. Marcy begin on private land. Crossing these lands with a firearm is prohibited at any time. During the big game season, hiking will not be allowed on these trails. For approximately six and one-half miles the route to Mt. Marcy is over private land where camping is not allowed. The red-marked trail starting from the parking lot one-half mile south of Elk Lake leads to Dix Mountain via Hunter Pass. Access from the gate to the trailhead parking area and beyond is closed during the big game hunting season.

The western approaches to the high peaks start at Tupper Lake. The trail begins at Coreys, which is reached by car after turning south from Route 3, the Tupper Lake-Saranac Lake Highway, about nine miles east of Tupper Lake Village. Automobiles may be driven seven miles further on the Amersand Road to the parking lot where the foot trail turns to the left for Marcy and the Cold River Country. The total distance to Marcy from Coreys is 33.4 miles.

The trail to Shattuck Clearing leads the hiker along the Calkins Creek Fire Trail to the Cold River at Shattuck Clearing. Here it connects with the blue-marked Northville-Placid trail.

Registration booths have been erected at important trail access points and junctions. Everyone using these trails is urged to sign these registers and give the additional information that is requested.

In the early 1890s guides developed a unique fixture in the Adirondacks called the lean-to. Ellsworth Petty developed the first shelter on Deer Island in Upper Saranac Lake. It proved so efficient that the Conservation Department standardized the dimensions at 10 feet by 16 feet to sleep 10 people, and added a fireplace, garbage

Adirondack lean-to displayed at the Adirondack Museum, typical of the hundreds of such shelters on the trails to the high peaks.

pit and a comfort station. It is made of spruce logs with three side walls, a sloping and over-hanging roof, and a plank floor with balsam bedding. It is cheap to make, using available materials for the most part, and is remarkably comfortable during an overnight rest period. There are at least 235 such lean-tos in the Adirondacks and about 134 are in the "high-peaks" region.

In recent years the high peaks have received extremely heavy use during the month of August and on holiday weekends, particularly Memorial Day, Labor Day and Columbus Day, often resulting in all lean-tos being occupied. It is wise for the cautious hiker and camper to carry rain gear and a tent for shelter.

If you visit the Adirondacks in winter use cross country skis or snowshoes on the trails. Wear them when traveling on soft or unpacked snow-covered trails. Many hiking trails are also used for ski travel. Boot holes in snow-covered trails are a safety hazard and make skiing difficult. If the trail is icy or hard-packed with snow, you may need crampons or creepers. You may also need a ski pole or an ice axe. If you are headed into mountainous country and you are skiing, don't forget to bring a spare tip in case you break a ski. You may need it to get out. You might also carry spare binding parts and a screw driver. Duct tape also helps with repairs. Carry a sleeping bag in case of possible injuries and a backpacker stove for warm drinks or food.

Don't let your clothing get wet, and try to stay warm. Snow shelters will get you out of the wind and usually will maintain a 32° temperature.

Other Hiking Trails

The high peaks offer the greatest challenge to hikers, but there are many other trails that are fun and rewarding. Perhaps the Siamese Ponds Wilderness is the best example. It comprises more then 112,000 acres or approximately 175 square miles of gentle mountains, lush forests, rushing streams and sparkling ponds. They are much less crowded than the mountainous wilderness areas to the north. The Siamese Ponds are an ideal destination for those seeking a true wilderness experience. But it is just one of many possibilities.

Hikers and campers should follow the guidelines established for maintaining these forest and mountain environments. What you carry in, carry out. Please leave the woods cleaner than you found them. It is wise to bring a refuse bag and carry out more than you carried in.

Much of the wildlife and plantlife leads a precarious existence, particularly in heavily-traveled areas. Leave them undisturbed so others can enjoy them.

If you plan to camp, carry your own tent in case the shelters are full. When you pitch your tent, place it on clear, level ground so you will disturb a minimum of ground cover. Much of it is fragile.

Wash your dishes and yourself at least 150 feet from and below all sources of drinking water. Waste water should be disposed of away from streams and springs. If there are no toilets nearby, dig a narrow trench 12 inches deep and 150 feet from water. Cover the trench completely when you break camp.

If you must build a fire, do so with care. Choose bare, level ground, clear away leaves and twigs for three feet, lay up stones and be sure the fire is completely out before you leave. It would be best if you brought a portable stove because this would save the wood supply. Be extra careful with cigarettes and matches.

It is important that you observe all posted regulations. Be considerate of fellow hikers and campers. Plan your trip carefully according to routes and the time available for your trip. Carry the latest guide books and maps. Always let someone know where you are going and when you expect to return. Groups of 10 or more require a camping permit. Smaller groups require one if camping over three nights in one location. Groups of six or fewer are preferred. Check the weather reports before you set out and be prepared for unexpected emergencies. Carry a compass, pocket knife, waterproof matches, high energy food such as candy, a first aid kit and extra protective clothing. In case of an accident, at least one person should remain with the injured person. Others should carefully note the location and contact the local forest ranger. Be sure to notify the ranger if any of your companions become lost. If you do become lost, keep calm, stay where you are and keep warm. If you believe you can try and find your way out, remember that following streams downhill will nearly always lead you back to habitation.

One final word of caution. As trail use increases, the number of dogs hiking with their masters is on the rise. Dog owners should exercise consideration toward fellow users of state lands so that restrictive measures will not be necessary for the control of pets. When others approach, particularly small children and other animals, leash your dog and keep him quiet. Under no circumstances should you permit your dog to make contact with drinkable water. Remember to remove droppings from the trail and campsite area. Keep your animal under control at all times. Others you meet have no knowledge of your dog's temperament, and they may react accordingly.

Hunting with a Camera

New York State has abundant rainfall, averaging more than 40 inches a year, so forests cover much of the land. Meadows have been created by people clearing land over the years, or where ground fires have occurred. For the non-hunter, they are an endless source of wonder at nature's miracles. Among the dozens of food chains that comprise a meadow's food web, a typical one transfers sun energy from grass blades to toad to garter snake to red-tailed hawk, as each is eaten by the next larger predator.

The summer months are the ideal time to go "meadow watching," particularly in the cool of the morning hours or early in the evening. You may not notice him immediately but a woodchuck has been watching you suspiciously as he stands on his hind legs on the dirt pile beside his hole. There are wild dogs in the woods, but coyotes are becoming more and more common. High above, hawks may be circling and occasionally you'll spot a narrow vee of Canada geese heading south.

Most meadows are privately owned but there are many such fields with public access, particularly at nearby state parks, nature centers and wildlife management areas. Most landowners will readily grant permission if you seek entry to their property. Be courteous and leave the area as unspoiled as the day you found it.

Autumn goes out in a blaze of color that is unmatched anywhere in the world. This is a last chance to get out and enjoy a lively session with a camera before winter sets in and turns the colorful woods into drab scenes of white, gray and green.

The source of autumn color provides a rich new food supply for some animals. Chipmunks eat their fill of newly fallen leaves before disappearing until spring into their dens with a cache of acorns for mid-winter snacks. Deer, their coats dull and thick, rely on both leaves and nuts from the trees to build up their winter fat reserves in preparation for the lean days ahead.

Chipmunks sleep on their stored food. Gray squirrels bury their acorns and hickory nuts one at a time. This practice achieves more than hiding food from other animals. In the ground they are protected from the harm of soaking and drying, freezing and the wind. In the spring uneaten nuts will germinate to begin their growth to sustain and spread the forest.

Just as tiny caterpillars feeding on expanding leaves fuel the spring flight of northbound songbirds, colorful fruit ripen in time for fall's southward flights. And the plants that feed migrating birds benefit in turn. In spring, they are spared from many ravenous insects. In fall, migrators spread the indigestible fruit seeds much farther than do year-round bird residents.

Brightly colored fruit advertises its presence to passers by. In order that red berries do not get lost among red autumn leaves, some plants have evolved other color combinations. Mocking birds pull ripe fruit from bright red stems of gray dogwoods. Wood thrush easily find the bluish-black fruit on arrowwood bushes. Crested flycatchers and catbirds eat fruit with an exaggerated color contrast of dark blue sassafras berries borne at one end of thick crimson fruit stems.

The popularity of beaver-felt hats in the 18th and 19th centuries came close to decimating the beaver population in New York State. Many of the state's earliest settlers subsisted on the fur trade. At one time the city of Albany was known as Beverwyck. By 1890 it was speculated that only 15 beaver remained in the state, probably in remote areas of the Adirondack Forest Preserve. Canadian and western beaver were introduced and beaver now can be found everywhere except in New York City and Long Island. Beaver can be destructive as well as useful residents. They help to create and rejuvenate wetlands that are home to many kinds of plants and animals. But beaver can cause road or real estate flooding with their dams. Despite their destructive habits, the beaver is New York State's official mammal.

Beaver are skittish animals and if you wish to catch them at work or play with your camera, it is best to approach a pond before dusk and sit quietly 50 to 70 feet from the water's edge. A good location would be near freshly-cut tree branches along the shore or in the water. As dusk approaches, the beaver should become active. Binoculars will help you to get a better look.

A beaver pond is a marvel of ingenuity, often flooding a sizable area and filled with drowned trees. Beavers keep their dams in good repair using only sticks and mud. Not all beaver build dams. Those that live along large streams and lakes do not. But you will notice their presence by the chewed and fallen trees surrounded by piles of large chips. You may find a beaver stick, with teeth marks at both ends, and the nutritious bark neatly chewed away. Beaver ponds are a source of endless delight for those with patience and perserverance.

Small Game Hunting

There are more than 3½ million acres of public land open to the hunter in New York State. This acreage includes farm fields, marshes, woodland and deep wilderness. In recent years turkey hunting has gained wide popularity because of the abundance of these wild birds. Marshlands provide an ideal habitat for ducks and geese. Ruffled grouse can often be found around the edges of old abandoned farm fields, as can cottontail rabbits. Snowshoe hare hunting challenges the endurance of winter hunters. In the Adirondacks a modest number of woodcock and grouse are found in rugged terrain and an even greater number of hare. Two and a quarter million of these acres are publicly owned and much of this is wilderness. The area has hundreds of lakes and streams and numerous beaver ponds. About 70% is woodland, with a mixture of hardwoods and conifers.

The transition zone in the Adirondack foothills is a rolling patchwork of woodlands, older thickets, swamp brushlots and abandoned farms. There are some small dairy farms in this area; most of the land is privately owned and may not be hunted or fished without permission. Grouse, woodcock and hare are frequently found in fair numbers, along with cottontail rabbits.

The season for all but gray squirrels and wild turkeys starts on October 1. Wild turkeys in this northern region can be hunted from October 1 through December; cottontail rabbits from October 1 through February. Ruffled grouse can be hunted from late September through February, woodcock in October and November only, and hare from October 1 to mid-March. The waterfowl season starts around October 1 and lasts through December.

Licenses

The New York State hunting license year starts on October 1 and lasts through September 30 of the following year. Keep these dates in mind if you are planning hunts in September.

Small game hunters must be 14 years of age. Those applying for licenses at ages 14 and 15 must have a proper license and show proof of having passed a certified hunter education course in the state of residence. They may hunt only when accompanied by a parent, guardian or designated person 18 or older who also has a current New York State license to hunt.

All residents and non-residents over 16 may hunt alone but must have a license. If you're from out of state, you may purchase a non-resident license if you show proof of a previous license either by showing the license itself or an affidavit from an issuing agent. If you've never had a license, proof of hunter education is necessary. The basic license costs $31 for residents and $35 for non-residents. These costs are often increased annually. Non-residents must pay $100 for a deer license. Youths 12-15 may hunt small game after they have successfully completed the basic firearm hunter education course but they must be accompanied while hunting by a qualified adult.

There's a special permit to hunt turkeys that costs $2. It entitles you to take one turkey during the fall season and two the following spring. If applying by mail, you may get the permit at the same time you purchase the small-game license. You can get your small-game license by writing the Department of Environmental Conservation's regional offices or the Town and County Clerks. Many sporting goods stores sell licenses. The easiest way for an out-of-stater to get one is to apply by mail. Send application requests to the New York State Department of Environmental Conservation, License Sales Office, Room 111, 50 Wolf Road, Albany, N.Y. 12233.

In order to legally hunt waterfowl, everyone 16 or over must have a federal migratory bird stamp, as well as a small-game license. The stamp may be purchased for $10 from most Post Offices. The federal stamp is not needed to hunt woodcock, snipe or rails.

Those who wish to carry a handgun in New York State must obtain a State Pistol Permit, which is issued only to residents. Be advised that permits from other states will not be honored!

Although the use of dogs during the spring turkey season is prohibited, it is advisable to use a good hunting dog for all other bird hunting and for cottontail rabbit and snowshoe hare hunting.

Please remember that you must have permission to hunt on private land. If the land is posted, it's essential that you obtain permission from the owners. The lack of posters does not give you automatic permission to trespass.

Waterfowl

New York has five waterfowl seasons and each one is tailored to the peak abundance of waterfowl in that particular region. Virtually every major waterfowl species of the Atlantic Flyway is here at one time or another during the four seasons. Some Adirondack beaver ponds are used in early season by blacks, mallards, woodies, widgeon and teal, just to name a few, but the Adirondacks and the Catskills offer limited opportunities to hunt waterfowl. There are many other places in the state where waterfowl hunting is exceptional and hunting for them in the Adirondacks and Catskills should not be considered unless part of other hunting activities. In these other regions, particularly those with large lakes and rivers and saltwater bays, out-of-state hunters need to be reminded that they should use a broad beamed boat at least 14 feet long with a minimum 7.5 horsepower motor. These waters can get very rough at times.

New York has more than 100,000 acres of prime wetlands in public ownership. Most of it is open to public hunting on a controlled basis. It is wise to know what these controls are so you won't be disappointed. Three reminders: steel shot is required state-wide for hunting waterfowl, and you must have both a federal duck stamp and a plug for your gun.

Big Game Hunting

Few places in the world surpass New York State for deer and bear hunting. There are 32,000 square miles of big game ranges where the deer population is among the largest in the United States. Within that complex there are 11,000 square miles of bear ranges. Even more remarkable is that 5,000 square miles of this entire area – roughly the size of Connecticut – is public land. For trophy buck hunting there's a rugged forestland of 10,000 square miles in the Adirondack Forest Preserve and nearly half of this land is publicly owned. This area also contains one of the largest black bear populations in the eastern United States.

Expressways connect all regions of New York State and bring hunters within a short distance of all kinds of big game hunting. For camping, there are two and a half million acres of Forest Preserve lands in the Adirondacks and you can select the camping conditions you like best.

In sharp contrast to big game hunting in the southern zone the northern zone, which includes the Adirondacks, offers an exciting variety of "low pressure" conditions ranging from rural to total wilderness, where you can enjoy the convenience of a motel or efficiency cabin, roadside camping or the true wilderness experience of backpacking into remote areas. Big game seasons are long, stretching from mid-September to early December. In addition to deer, this region has 90% of New York's 4,100 black bears.

There are substantially fewer deer in the northern zone than in the southern zone because of range quality and winter severity. But hunting pressure is less. Only 30% of the bucks taken in the state are taken in the Adirondacks. Therefore your chances of success are equally good throughout the season. If you're looking for "big racks" you'll find them in the remote sections of the Adirondacks. This is due to the lower rate of buck harvesting, resulting in an overall older age of bucks in the Adirondacks.

These remote areas include the extremely rugged terrain in the "high peaks" region, where elevations rise to 5,300 feet. Ninety percent of this area is forested and 90% is in public ownership. Road access is limited, but hiking trails are common. In the central Adirondacks, mountains rise to 4,000 feet and much of this area is wilderness. Many of the lakes and streams can be navigated by boat or canoe.

The regular season for white-tailed deer (bucks only) and bear in the Adirondacks starts in October and lasts through December. The archery season starts September 27 and ends October 22. The muzzleloading season begins October 16, lasting until October 21.

Big game hunters who want to take a bobcat or coyote must have a small game hunting license. The pelt must be tagged according to procedures required for taking small game. For these animals the Furbearer Possession Tag must be used.

All residents who hunt deer and bear must have a big game, sportsman's or junior archery license. During the archery season, a bow-hunting stamp must also be attached to the validated license. Persons hunting deer or bear with a longbow during the regular season must possess a current bow-hunting stamp or a valid bow-hunter education certificate. Please note that the use of barbed broadhead arrowheads is illegal. During the muzzleloading season, a muzzleloading stamp also must be attached to the validated license. All non-residents in the state who hunt deer or bear must have a non-resident license.

Persons applying for a big game license must show proof of qualification. This can be a hunting license previously issued to the applicant from another state or country, or a hunter education certificate issued to the applicant.

Applications must be postmarked no later than September 10 to be included in the first round of permit selection. Applications postmarked between September 11 and 17 will be processed only if permits are still available. Those postmarked later than September 17 will not be processed.

Persons 14 or 15 years of age may hunt big game with bow and arrow under the authority of a junior archery license but only during the archery season or during the regular season in areas restricted to bowhunting. To obtain a junior archery license, both the bow and firearms hunter education courses must be completed. They must be accompanied by a licensed big game hunter (with archery stamp affixed to license) at least 18 years old with at least one year of big game hunting experience using bow and arrow.

Persons under the age of 16 may not hunt big game with firearms. Those 16-17 years of age must be accompanied by a licensed big game hunter at least 18 years old with at least one year of big-game hunting experience. The Junior Hunting License may be used only to hunt small game.

Active members of the United States Armed Forces stationed in New York State, and full-time college students who are American citizens residing in the state during the school year qualify for resident licenses, but they must provide proof.

Lifetime licenses are available and they are an especially good buy for children under 12 because of the reduced rate. The license is valid for the holder's lifetime. Even after moving out of the state resident sporting privileges are retained.

Licenses may be purchased by mail using a standard license application available from the regional office of the Department of Environmental Conservation. These should be sent to the New York State Department of Environmental Conservation, License Sales Office, Room 111, 50 Wolfe Road, Albany, N.Y. 12233-4790.

There are certain restrictions that must be observed while hunting in New York State. It is unlawful to carry or possess a shotgun or rifle in or on a motor vehicle unless both chamber and magazine are unloaded. There are restrictions about using lights where deer are present, the discharge of a firearm or longbow within 500 feet of a dwelling, school, playground or an occupied factory or church. In general no non-resident may carry a handgun in New York State, and restrictions are tight for residents.

A person who kills a deer by law must mail in the "duplicate" Deer Report portion of his big game tags within 10 days after the deer is killed. A bear killed must be reported in two ways. First a person taking a bear must report the kill by calling toll-free (800) 342-9832 within 24 hours of reaching a road and before the bear is transported out of state. Second, the person must also fill out and mail within five days after the close of the bear season the reverse side of the Bear Report portion of the currently valid big game tags, or the non-resident bear tag.

These reports are important to state officials for the better management of the deer and bear population, and to assure that the "kills" are not excessive. It is evident that the deer population has been increasing steadily after several mild winters in the state, although the winter of 1993/1994 proved to be one of the worst in the last half-century.

When traveling in the Adirondacks it is wise to bring a compass and a topographic map and know how to use them. Weather conditions in fall and winter can change from mild to severe overnight. Dress warmly and carry fire starters, waterproof matches, flashlights and high energy foods. In the event you become lost, don't panic. Stay in one place and build a smokey fire. The Forest Rangers will soon find you. If a member of your party is overdue, seek help.

Many people employ professional guides, and this can be a wise decision. Guides are licensed by the state so you can depend upon them. A list of such guides can be obtained by writing the Department of Environmental Conservation and Fire Management, 50 Wolf Road, Room 414, Albany, N.Y. 12233.

Fishing

When anglers think of New York's Adirondack Mountain area, it's mostly in terms of trout. But there are 350 major lakes, including 314,000-acre Lake Champlain, with great fishing for bass, pike, pickerel, walleye and even muskie.

You can tour the Saranac Lake system, passing through antique, hand-operated locks, camp on island campsites at Lake George, Indian Lake and Saranac Lake. You can pitch a tent anywhere on state lands which border most Adirondack waters. Or you can stay at the finest tourist accommodations, which are always nearby.

One of the best times to fish these waters is in early fall in northern New York when the trees and hillsides are ablaze with autumn colors. You'll probably be the only person on the water.

Small mouth bass are the most common gamefish, but there are waters with large mouth, too. Big bass can be found in Lake Champlain, Lake George, Long Lake and the Saranac lakes. Northern pike are abundant in many Adirondack lakes and rivers and there are some walleye hot spots in Lake Champlain and the Raquette River system. Yellow perch, bullheads and sun fish are plentiful in most waters, and southern Lake Champlain yields outstanding channel catfish and crappie.

Every New York region offers excellent fishing for tough, rod-bending small mouth bass. They inhabit more than one million acres of lakes, ponds and streams. One- to two-pound small mouths are abundant, and two- to three-pound fish are common. Even six- to eight-pound trophy fish are caught each year. Typically, New York's bass waters are uncrowded, making for a special kind of fishing pleasure.

Try still fishing and/or drifting with minnows and crayfish or troll and cast with small plugs, jigs and spinners. You'll find the small mouths in shallow waters in the spring and fall, but they move into deeper waters in mid-summer.

Large mouth bass are widespread in New York, occurring in almost every major lake, in countless ponds and a surprising number of rivers and streams. Many waters are lightly fished and you may surprise yourself by hooking an old lunker. Each year seven- to 10- pound large mouth bass are taken. More common, however, are those weighing one to three pounds. They'll test your tackle and skill with a rod. You're more likely to find them in shallow areas where there's some cover over the water and among weed beds. Use plastic worms, spinner baits, plugs, jigs, top-water lures or live bait.

Bullheads aren't much to look at, but some consider them a delicacy. They're plentiful in the springtime and easy to catch. You'll probably find them on the bottom, and a worm on a hook with a slip sinker should entice them to your line. Lake Champlain is one of several areas in the northeast where abundant catches of bullheads are possible. In May, warm shallow bays and tributaries offer large concentrations for anglers. Catches of 30 bullheads an hour are not uncommon.

Muskellunge are found in only one place in the Adirondacks and that's in the Great Chazy River in Clinton County. It takes even a veteran angler 10 hours or more to catch one of these huge fish. They can average 12 to 30 pounds. The record fish was caught in the St. Lawrence and weighed 69 pounds, 15 ounces. Special fishing gear is required and a guide is recommended if you're serious about catching one of these tackle-busting monsters.

The walleye can put up an exciting light-tackle fight. It is one of the most delicious of all gamefish, with a delicate flavor. New York walleyes average one to three pounds, but some weigh up to 15 pounds. They're found in 89 of the state's lakes and in 10 of its major river systems. Favored Adirondack spots include: Blake and Carry Falls reservoirs in St. Lawrence County, Great Sacandaga Lake in Fulton and Saratoga counties, Higley Flow in St. Lawrence County, Lincoln Pond in Hamilton County and Rainbow Falls Reservoir in St. Lawrence County, Sacandaga Reservoir in Hamilton County, Tupper Lake and Union Falls Flow in Franklin County, the Hudson, Raquette and St. Regis rivers. A permit is required from the St. Regis Indian Tribe to fish the lower St. Regis River. Whether it's open-water fishing along a winding, tree-lined river or ice fishing on a snow-blanketed lake, you'll find fast walleye action in New York State.

Northern pike are found in most lakes and rivers in the Adirondacks. They are known for their vicious strikes. In large lakes and rivers outside the Adirondacks they will weigh between 15 and 20 pounds. In the Adirondacks they are much smaller, although they are just as scrappy. Use large spoons, plugs, spinners and live bait and be prepared for some heavy action.

The thrill and beauty of a fresh-caught trout in the seclusion of a remote Adirondack pond is an experience you won't forget. There are hundreds of these ponds and lakes in the ancient Adirondacks. Some are by the roadside while others are miles from the nearest highway. Brook trout thrive in cool, clear streams with an average weight between three and four pounds in ponds, and 12 to 14 inches long in streams. You can catch them on flies, spinners, spoons and worms.

Lake trout are normally found in deep lakes but you'll find them in shallow water during the cool months of spring and fall. You can fish for them through the ice in the winter because they feed the year round. Use tip-ups with minnows in winter. In open water cast or troll with spoons or plugs. You can still fish with live bait.

Rainbow trout are not as plentiful in the Adirondacks as they are in the rest of the state. Go for surface trolling and shore fishing in spring and fall, deepwater trolling in summer, and ice fishing in winter.

Brown trout are more plentiful around the periphery of the Adirondacks. They run about 15 inches in length and are known for their elusiveness. Flies, spinners and natural baits are the most effective.

The silvery, hook-throwing leaps of landlocked salmon are legendary. They are not abundant, and are found principally in Lake Champlain, Lake George and Schroon Lake. In the spring and fall, surface trolling works best, with deep water trolling in mid-summer. Fly-casting in fall spawning streams is effective, as are tip-ups in winter. Spoons, plugs and flies that imitate smelt are effective lures.

Salmon and trout fishing in Lake Champlain can be done throughout the year but there is a daily limit for these species. Trout must be a minimum length of 12 inches and only three can be taken in a day. Lake trout are limited to 15 inches and only three can be kept. Landlocked salmon must be 15 inches long; you are limited to two daily.

In Lake Champlain, landlocks seem to prefer Mooselock wobblers in the small or medium size in brass, copper or fluorescent red, while trolled at a fast speed on downriggers or lead core line. Rapalas, dodger/fly combinations, and various types of spoons are also effective. Salmon and brown trout seem to concentrate in the deep water area from Westport north to Split Rock in late August and September.

Walleyes are commonly taken by fishermen trolling for trout and salmon, especially from late May to early August. You'll find them suspended over deep water during daylight hours and, as dusk approaches, they follow smelt to the surface. The period from dusk to midnight is a favorite time for fishing walleyes. Flatfish in U-20 and larger sizes and joined Rapalas or Rebels are favorite lures.

For up-to-date information, call the fishing hotlines in Warrensburg at (518) 623-3682 or Ray Brook at (518) 891-5413, 24 hours a day, seven days a week. Local bait and tackle shops along the lake can also provide helpful information.

A New York fishing license is restricted to New York waters of Lake Champlain. A Vermont license is necessary to fish in Vermont waters of the lake. The New York/Vermont line is roughly mid-lake in the Willsboro Point, Essex and Westport areas of Champlain. Fishing regulations are subject to change, so it would be wise to consult the New York State Department of Environmental Conservation's Regional Law Enforcement Office at Ray Brook, (518) 891-1370, for up-to-date information.

Licenses

Everyone who fishes in New York State waters must have a fishing license, except those under 16 years of age, those fishing on licensed fishing preserves and active members of the United States Armed Forces who are New York State residents and are in the state for a maximum of 30 days. Letter writers must identify themselves with ID cards or furlough papers. Free licenses may be obtained by patients of United States Veterans Administration hospitals, Department of Mental Hygiene institutions and Department of Health rehabilitation centers. Application must be made to the License Sales Office, Room 111, 50 Wolf Road, Albany, N.Y. 12233-4790.

New York residents pay $14 for a fishing license and there is a special three-day license for residents that costs $6. The non-resident license is $28, with a five-day charge of $16. The license year starts on October 1 and ends on September 30.

Trapping

Trapping of fur-bearing animals in the Adirondacks is done primarily by professionals starting on October 1 for the next 12 months, depending upon the region.

All persons who trap wildlife such as beaver, fisher, otter and pine marten in the state must have a trapping license or junior trapping license except for resident owners, leasees and members of their immediate families, and Indian resident owners and resident members of their immediate families when trapping on farm land occupied and cultivated by them. Indians who live on reservations do not need a trapping license. Members of the United States Armed Forces who are stationed elsewhere and are in the state no longer than 30 days do not need licenses but they must have proof of active service.

There are many laws and restrictions that control trapping in New York, including regions by dates, types of traps, and a host of general regulations such as tagging of carcasses. Contact the Department of Environmental Conservation for a brochure called "Trapping Guide." There are a number of regional offices. For the Adirondacks and Catskills write Region Four, 2176 Guilderland Avenue, Schenectady, N.Y. 12306-4496. Or call (518) 382-0680.

Rabies

R abies in raccoons has been confirmed in many counties in southern, central and western New York. An outbreak of fox rabies has been reported in parts of northern New York in Franklin, Clinton and Essex counties. Trappers should take special precautions to avoid the risk of exposure to this often fatal disease.

All people visiting or living in wild areas should avoid animals that act strangely, especially those that are unusually tame, aggressive or paralyzed. Everyone should be suspicious of daytime activity by raccoons, skunks and foxes that normally are active at night.

When skinning a fur-bearing animal, it is prudent to wear rubber gloves and eye protection since the virus may be transmitted in any body fluid. This means that the virus could enter a cut or scratch, or travel through a mucous membrane in the eyes, nose or mouth.

If you believe you have been exposed to a rabid animal, wash the wound thoroughly with soap and water and seek medical attention immediately. Try to capture or kill the animal without damaging the head. Preserve the dead animal by refrigeration as soon as possible, and contact your local health office.

The Adirondacks is a land of extremes, but one like no other place on earth. Its woods are overflowing with animal life, and its sparsely-settled regions await the adventurous. Some people never go beyond the places that can be reached by automobile, but those who make the effort to get off the beaten path will marvel at the region's diversity and enchanting vistas. But do not go alone and be prepared and knowledgeable because this is still a wilderness that can quickly turn a happy holiday into a tragedy.

The Catskills

History

The Catskills were a level plateau in pre-glacial times, rising above a sea that covered much of the surrounding region. The mountains today show the results of weathering, stream erosion, and outwardly-moving valley glaciers associated with the continental ice sheets of 20,000 to 50,000 years ago. The sandstones and other rocks of the Catskills, now exposed by cliffs and gorges, have long given geologists a unique chance to study significant records of the rock system of Devonian times. Vertebrate fossils – bony fragments of early jawless fish – date back 450 million years. In the Devonian period, during the Age of Fishes about 350 million years ago, the vertebrates multiplied. Five classes of fish had evolved by the Devonian period, including jawless fish, represented today only by the parasite lampreys and bagfish, the jewel armored fishes, and the spiny "sharks" which are both extinct. True sharks, skates and rays and the bony fish complete the classes.

These vertebrates later became fish, amphibious reptiles, birds and mammals. It is now known that these vertebrate pioneers who moved from the sea to land were not the first inhabitants. Fossil evidence indicates that plants and arthropods (invertebrate animals such as insects, arachnids, and crustaceans that have a disjointed body and limbs) had earlier migrated to land. These plants had no true roots or leaves and were little more than a bundle of tubes. By the Devonian Period small plants were growing in abundance.

In the 1860s a flash flood in the Catskills exposed fossil "tree stumps" that had grown in Devonian times. While excavating for a dam later, more stumps were revealed. Quite possibly this is the earth's first known forest. In what obviously was a large area of trees, some 30 feet tall, they had tapered trunks crowned by long, green, leaflike fronds.

The Catskills are a section of the Appalachian Plateau. They are characterized by bulky masses between summits with only a few valleys. Deep gorges called "cloves" are filled with magnificent waterfalls. The rivers and streams drain in three directions: northward to the Mohawk River by Schoharie Creek; eastward to the Hudson River by Esopus, Catskill and other creeks, and southwestward to the Delaware River by headstreams of that river that flow from the Catskills. Ashokan Reservoir on Esopus Creek and Schoharie Reservoir are part of the New York City water supply system. The sloping summits, all heavily forested, are clearly visible from the shores of the Hudson River. They are a striking sight. The highest peak is Slide Mountain, with an elevation of 4,204 feet.

Henry Hudson discovered the Catskills in 1609 as he voyaged up the Hudson River in the *Half Moon*. Within a decade the Dutch settled the area, leaving their influence in many ways down to the present, although the British took control of the region in the 1660s.

No great battles were fought in the Catskills and most of its history is fairly modern. There are many historic sites, such as the Senate House in Kingston, which was built in 1676 and where the first session of the New York State Senate was held in 1777. The Bronck House Museum was built in 1663. It is the former home of Jonas Bronck for whom the Bronx, one of New York City's five boroughs, was named. The Hasbrouck Memorial House, built in New Paltz in 1772, is one of several Huguenot houses in the city. The birthplace of nature writer John Burroughs and of financier Jay Gould at Roxbury may be of interest. Palenville, the legendary home of Rip Van Winkle, hero of Washington Irving's short story by the same name, attracts thousands each year. Since 1900 Woodstock has been a colony of artists, writers and musicians.

The Catskills are primarily a resort area and vacationland for year-round tourists. There are state camping sites, a state ski center at Belleayre Mountain with miles of trout streams and a network of hiking paths. The Catskill Forest Preserve covers approximately 700,000 acres. New York State owns about 40% of it.

Today it is a largely rural area with industries that produce business machines, electrical machinery, clothing, processed foods, and stone, clay and glass products. Superhighways link the area to New York City and the rest of the state. Dairying, fruit farming and poultry raising are the main agricultural products.

Access

Indians called the Catskills Onteora or "land in the sky." Today you can reach this popular resort area by taking one of four routes from the Hudson Valley. State Route 23 and 23A leave the town of Catskill and ascend the steep 1,000-foot wall of the Catskills' eastern edge. The ski resort of Windham is reachable through here but the road itself continues on beyond the Catskills to Oneonta. State Route 23A passes by the Kasterskill Falls, which plunge down the face of a 180-foot gorge. Then it joins State Route 23 at Prattsville. State Route 28 leaves Kingston and passes the Ashokan Reservoir before traveling into the heart of the Catskills. There the road traverses the least developed part of the mountain preserve. State Route 17 between Harriman State Park and I-87 and Binghamton provides access to some resort towns in the Catskills. Monticello is popular with tourists who wish to explore the headwaters of the Delaware River.

What to See & Do

The Catskills Forest Preserve is only 90 miles from New York City, and less than 300 miles from the Adirondacks. It is most beautiful in June when the laurel blooms, and in October when the leaves turn. Here are located the Beaver Kill, Neversink and Willowemoc, three of the best fishing streams in the state.

There are a growing number of bed and breakfast places offering hospitality unobtainable in the more commercial hotels and inns. Throughout the area there are quaint towns nestled in the scenic Catskill Mountains. Sullivan County, along the magnificent Delaware River, has a particularly fine recreation, shopping and dining facilities. There are first class golf courses, fresh water lakes, world-renowned fishing streams, as well as hunting and skiing areas.

The Catskills have long been known as a quiet and scenic region – an unsurpassed playground for adults and children, with canoeing, rafting, horseback riding, flying and skiing, to name just a few of the activities available.

Soaring is enjoyed by the more adventurous at Wurtsboro Airport on Route 209. It is the oldest soaring site in the United States and is located along the southern edge of the Shawangunk Mountains. It is open daily, weather permitting, for rides or lessons. For details, call 888-2791 from 8:30 a.m. to 5:00 p.m.

Kayacking on the white-water streams in the Catskills can test your spirit of adventure. Thrill-a-minute rides down swift streams, dodging rocks along the way, requires some skill as well as enthusiasm.

Shopping is an all-American pastime and the Catskills is an ideal place to buy about everything imaginable. There are fine antiques, and arts and crafts that can be purchased from country boutiques or wholesale bargain outlets. Parksville has four large showrooms filled with beautiful antiques in classic and antique styles. Some of these memorabilia date back to 1820.

An authentic country fair, the **Little World's Fair** at Grahamsville Fairgrounds is a wonderful family outing with more than 400 exhibits. There are rides, games and country music for all ages. It takes place August 13, 14 and 15.

The colorful **Ukrainian Youth Festival** in Glen Spey offers diverse entertainment on July 16, 17 and 18. It is filled with music, laughter and dancing and it is held annually.

Fort Delaware in on Route 97 at Narrowsburg. It's a replica of an early settlement on the scenic Delaware River. Special colonial demonstrations and exhibits are open to the public starting on May 29. In June it is open on weekends, and daily in late June until Labor Day. There is a modest admission charge, with family and group rates.

The **Monticello Raceway** has races year round, with admission only $1.50 and free parking. This is one of the fastest tracks in the nation for pari-mutuel racing. There are three daily doubles. Dinner is available in the Club Escoffier, the glass-enclosed grandstand or tiered seating overlooking the track. You can reach the track by taking Exit 104 off Route 17B in Monticello.

Sullivan County is the winter home for more than 100 bald eagles. They seek the open reservoir and rivers, with their abundance of fish.

There are a number of private preserves in the Catskills. One of the most popular is the **Eldred**, which is open year round on a 2,500-acre outdoor resort facility. It caters to fishermen and hunters while providing fine food and excellent lodging facilities. Eldred has two bass lakes that are among the 25 best places to fish in the United States. Daily rates, including two people in a boat, are $60 for an eight-hour day.

Three stream-fed ponds are located on the preserve. They are open year round and stocked with rainbow, brown, brook and golden trout. The admission charge is $2.50 per person, and an additional charge of $3.90 a pound for the fish you catch.

Big and small game hunting is available on 600 acres. The Eldred Preserve is noted for its deer and turkey hunting.

The club offers 12-month memberships at reduced savings. The prices start at $100 and range up to $500. The latter provides unlimited hunting and admission to trout ponds, 20 rounds of sporting clays, six days of boat rentals on the bass lakes and a 10% discount on other facilities.

Guests stay in one of 21 log-cabin-style rooms that are maintained in a rustic setting. Prices range from $68 to $75 in season, and $55 to $65 out of season. A mid-week bass fishing package is $75 for a room and boat rental. New York State taxes are additional.

An adjacent four-star restaurant serves full dinners on an à la carte basis. Their banquet hall serves 175 people.

The Eldred Preserve can be reached by taking the Thruway (Route 87) from New York City or Albany. From New York go over the Tappan Zee Bridge and get off at Exit 16 at Harriman. Take Route 17 to Exit 104 (Monticello Raceway) and follow Route 17B straight through a blinker light at White Lake and turn left on to Route 55 West. Eldred is eight miles farther on the left hand side. From Albany get off the Thruway at Exit 19 and go southwest on Route 209, then pick up Route 17 and proceed according to instructions for the New York City access route.

Every spring Delaware River anglers eagerly await arrival of the annual spawning of the American shad. Shad spend most of their lives in the Atlantic Ocean until they are three to five years old and weigh over five pounds. Then they return to the Delaware River in which they were born to spawn. The peak of the shad run is generally in May, with adult shad present in the river through June and even into late July in some years.

The traditional opening of the trout season is April 1. The Willowemoc, the Beaverkill and the Delaware River won't disappoint you. Of interest to many fishermen is the **Catskill Fly Fishing Center**, which is open all year. This 35-acre site on the Willowemoc has hundreds of meticulously crafted flies, rods, reels and priceless artifacts from past and present masters of the art.

Students attending the education program become well-versed in entomology, water testing, acid rain and stream improvement, in addition to developing their angling skills.

The center is easily reached from Route 17, Exit 94 at Roscow or Exit 96 at Livingston Manor. Summer hours are 10:00 a.m. to 4 p.m. daily, April through September. Winter hours are Monday through Friday 9:00 a.m. to 1:00 p.m., except on holidays. For further information write Catskill Fly Fishing Center, R.D. #1, Box 130C, Livingston Manor, New York, 12758. Or call (914) 439-4810.

Ski Windham, a family-oriented ski area with 33 trails and seven ski lifts, is off Route 23. Open year round, its winter programs include the Children's Learning Center and Ski School and the Disabled Ski Program. During summer and fall there are antique shows, craft fairs, country fairs and flea markets. Mountain biking is popular, along with trail riding. It is open daily April-October from 8 a.m. to 5 p.m., Monday through Friday. The rest of the year it is open on Saturday, Sunday, and holidays from 8 a.m. to 4 p.m. Lift tickets on Saturday, Sunday and holidays are priced at $35; ages 7-12, $29; Monday through Friday, $26; but $23 for ages 7-12 and $13 for those over 65. Call toll-free (800) 729-7549.

In Prattsville, the home of its founder and United States Representative **Zadock Pratt** is now a museum on Main Street. The house dates back to 1828 and contains original and period furniture as well as the town's history. It is open Wednesday-Sunday from 1 p.m. to 5 p.m. and on Memorial Day and Columbus Day. Admission is $2, or 50¢ for those under 13.

Kingston is one of the oldest communities in the United States. The Dutch established a trading post there in 1614 and it became a permanent settlement in 1652. New York's first constitution was drafted there and adopted in 1777 when the city became the first capital. There are many colonial homes in Kingston, most notably the **Bevier House** that now serves as Ulster County's Historical Society Headquarters and Museum.

You can take walking tours on your own through the historic **Uptown Stockade** and the **Midtown and Rondout Creek Corridor**, guided by directions in brochures obtainable at Kingston's City Hall, 1 Garraghan Drive. Their phone number is (914) 331-0080.

The **Ashokan Reservoir** lies west in the Catskills. It is encircled by a picturesque 40-mile drive on State Routes 28 and 28A. The reservoir normally supplies 500 million gallons of water daily for New York City.

The **Old Dutch Church and Cemetery** is on Main Street between Wall and Fair Streets. It was established in 1659, and the cemetery two years later. The latter contains the grave of George Clinton, New York's first governor. They are open Monday-Friday from 9 a.m. until 4 p.m. or by appointment. There's no charge. The phone number is (914) 338-6759.

The **Senate House State Historic Site** is at 312 Fair Street and marks the place where New York State's Senate first met. There are exhibits on the formation of the New York State government and displays about Hudson Valley artists. The rooms appear just as they were in 1777. There are guided tours Wednesday through Saturday from 10 a.m. to 5 p.m., and Sunday from 1 p.m. to 5 p.m., April 15-October 31. The tours are free.

The Trolley Museum of New York is at 89 E. Strand Street in the Kingston Urban Cultural Park. Take Exit 19 off I-87 to Colonel Chandler Drive to Broadway and then to Rondout Creek. This museum is dedicated to rapid-rail transit. You can take a one-and-a-half-mile trolley ride on the Old Ulster & Delaware Railroad track along the Hudson River. Be sure and visit the museum. It is open Friday-Sunday and holidays from noon until 5 p.m., Memorial Day-Columbus Day. A trolley ride is $2 but half that price for ages 1-14. For details, call (914) 331-3399.

Where to Stay

The Aladdin Hotel at Woodbourne has 200 rooms and is open May-October. Its Jewish-American cuisine is on the American Plan. There are indoor-outdoor pools, a sauna, a health club, two all-weather tennis courts, two shuffle-board courts, fishing on premises, free bridge and dance lessons and nightly entertainment. Bungalows and efficiency units include linen, maid service, china and silver. Rooms are air conditioned and heated. The summer weekly rate is $250-$335 per person, double occupancy. The weekend rate is $50-$60 a day. For reservations call (914) 434-4096 or (212) 354-0343.

The Albergo Allegria Country Inn is on State Route 296. From State Route 23 drive a tenth of a mile south from Windham. From Friday and Saturday 12/15-12/31, the rate is $95-$125. From Friday and Saturday 3/2-12/14, the rate is $65-$95. Sunday-Thursday 12/15-3/1, the rate for two persons, one bed is $65-$95. Sunday-Thursday, 3/2-12/14, the rate is $45-$85. No pets are allowed. For reservations write Route 296, Box 267, Windham 124-96, or call (518) 734-5560.

Best Western Monticello is on State Route 178, a quarter-mile south of its junction with State Route 17, Exit 17. Friday and Saturday from 5/21-9/6 the rate is $85-$95. Sunday through

Thursday 5/21-9/6 the rate is $75-$85. For reservations, write Best Western at 21 Raceway Road, Monticello, 12701, or call (914) 796-4000.

The Blue Spruce Bed and Breakfast at Cochecton is a 1900 vintage farm house that is open all year and can be reached off Route 17B on County Road 114 from Fosterdale. It is between Monticello and the Delaware River on Route 97. No pets are allowed and in-house smoking is not permitted. The rates are $55 single and $65-$75 double and these rates include full country breakfast. There are facilities nearby for dining, fishing, skiing, golfing, horseback riding, hunting and canoeing. For reservations write 580 CR 114, Cochecton, New York, 12726 or call (914) 8236.

Carl's Rip Van Winkle Motor Lodge in Catskill has 37 units. It is on County Road 23B, a quarter-mile west of I-87's Exit 21. It is open from 4/7-11/7 and offers motel rooms and log cabins on a wooded hillside. The rooms are $42-$55. Cabins rent weekly in season for $400-$425 for up to four persons. No pets. For reservations, write HC 2, Box 45, Leeds 12414 or call (518) 943-3303.

Concord Resort Hotel at Kiamesha Lake is a few miles north of Monticello. It has 1,200 rooms and is open year-round except for December 7-20. There's a new show nightly with no cover or minimum charge and meals are served under all plans. There are 45 holes of golf on the premises, indoor and outdoor tennis courts, and a full range of indoor and outdoor sports. The European Plan starts at $65 a day and others are commensurate. For reservations write Concord Resort Hotel, Kiamesha Lake, New York, 12751, or call toll-free (800) 431-3850.

The Fosterdale Heights House is open year-round. It is an 1840 bed and breakfast house with 12 guest rooms, a Victorian parlor, and a wrap-around porch. Peaceful and quiet, it is surrounded by acres of Christmas trees and forest. Located off route 17B between Monticello and the Delaware River, it is restricted to adults, and pets are not allowed. It charges $56 a night for a couple. Dinner is available on Friday and Saturday. For reservations, write to 205 Mueller Road, Fosterdale, NY 12726 or call (914) 482-3369.

Geronimo's Resort and Conference Center in Walker Valley has 33 rooms in a cozy mountain top inn. It is on the American plan and the indoor and outdoor pools are heated. There are facilities for tennis, and skiing packages can be arranged. The rate is $90 per person double occupancy. For reservations, write Box 155, Walker Valley, N.Y. 12588.

The Guest House in Livingston Manor is on the banks of the Willowemoc River, long known as a hangout for the rich and famous. Fishing, hunting, swimming and almost all outdoor sports are possible on its 40 acres. Each room has a private bath. Breakfast is served and there is a complimentary afternoon English tea plus pre-dinner refreshments. Rooms are priced from $100 to $200 a day and it is open all year. For reservations, write The Guest House, 223 Debruce Road, Livingston Manor, N.Y. 12758 or call (914) 439-4000.

Hills Summer Resort at Callicoon Center has 60 rooms that are rented May-September under the American Plan. There's an outdoor pool, tennis courts, and entertainment on weekends. There are nearby facilities for horseback riding, golfing and canoeing. The weekly rate in summer is $350-$400 per person for double occupancy. Weekends the rate is $65-$70 per person, double occupancy. For reservations call (914) 482-9885 or write P.O. Box 63, Callicoon Center, N.Y. 12724.

The Howard Johnson Lodge can be reached from State Route 17, Exit 109, a half-mile east of the old State Route 17, or Rock Hill Road. It is open all year with a single rate of $49-$89; two persons with one or two beds for $55-$89. For reservations, write the Lodge at 190 Broadway, Monticello 12701 or call (914) 796-3000.

Koch's Restaurant on County Route 23B is a half-mile west of I-87 and serves American and some German food. It is open 5/1-10/18 from 4 p.m. to 8 p.m. and Sunday from 11 a.m. For reservations, call (518) 943-5340.

The Huff House at Roscoe has 47 rooms and is open from April 30-October 21. It operates under the American Plan. There's an outdoor heated pool, spring-fed, stocked trout pond, and a nine-hole golf course. World famous trout streams are nearby. There are pet restrictions and reservations are required. The rates are $105 per person. The weekly rate is $510-$555 per person. For reservations, call toll-free (800) 243-4567, or write the Huff House, Roscoe, N.Y. 12776.

Lagriglia Restaurant serves northern Italian food and it can be reached by taking State Route 23, then driving a tenth of a mile south on State Route 296. It is open 11:30 a.m.-3 p.m., and 4 p.m.-10 p.m. For reservations call (518) 734-4499.

La Conca D'Oro Restaurant is in the center of Catskill at 440 Main Street and serves Italian food. It is open 11:30 a.m. to 10 p.m. but with only dinner schedules on Saturday and Sunday. It is closed on Tuesday. For reservations write the address above or call (518) 943-3549.

The Leeds County Inn is open 5/1-10/31 on State Route 23B, two miles west of I-87 and Exit 21. A single room is $35-$42 and a double with two persons is $40-$54. No pets. For reservations write HC 2, Box 45, Leeds, 12414, or call (518) 943-3303.

The Logsider Cafe is close to Carl's Rip Van Winkle Motor Lodge. It is closed on Wednesday and from 1/2-2/13.

M & M's Country House in Glen Wild is a 150-year-old country house situated on 20 wooded acres. Only 90 minutes from New York City, it offers suites with jacuzzi and private bath, two-room suites with private baths and one two-bedroom housekeeping apartment. The price of the rooms start at $65, which includes a country breakfast. There's swimming, skiing, golfing, horseback riding and a host of other things. For reservations write Mike

Mohonk Lake, adjoining Mohonk Mountain House in the Catskills.

Thompson, P.O. Box 673, Glen Wild Road, Glen Wild, N.Y. 12738 or call (914) 434-2716 or (212) 495-6486.

The Mohonk Mountain House is world famous and is only 90 miles from New York City. It can be reached by taking Exit 18 off I-87, then driving two miles west to Springtown Road and four miles north following the signs. The rates are: one person, $160-$225; two persons, one bed, $250-$325; and two persons, two beds $255-$340. These rates are based on the American Plan, which includes meals. A wide variety of indoor and outdoor recreational activities are available. Pets are not allowed. There are three dining rooms and the setting for the Mountain House is incredibly beautiful. For reservations, call (914) 255-4500 or write to 1,000 Mountain Rest Home, 12561.

The Red Ranch Motel is open 6/18-9/6 and 11/24-4/1. It is on Route 32, a half-mile south of the junction to State Route 23A at Exit 20 off I-87. Drive nine miles north of Route 32 to number 4555. In summer and fall the rates are $45 for two persons and one bed, or

$45-$65 for two persons, two beds. For spring and winter the rates are $34 for two persons one bed, and $38-$49 for two persons, two beds. For reservations write the motel at 4555 Route 32, 12414, or call (518) 678-3380.

South Wind Hotel at Woodbourne has 60 rooms and is open from mid-June to Labor Day. It operates on the American Plan with three meals a day. There is an outdoor pool and a lake nearby for swimming, row-boating and fishing. Pets are not allowed. Weekly rates range from $225-$260 per person, double occupancy. For reservations call (914) 434-5032 or write Box 60, Budd Road, Woodbourne, N.Y. 12788.

The Sunny Oaks Hotel at Woodbridge has 50 rooms and is open from June 15 to September 15. Dining is on the American Plan. There's folk, round and line dancing most evenings. The single rate is $42-$82 and double occupancy per person is $44-$57. The nearby motel rates for June and September are $25-$40 and double occupancy $30-$50. For reservations write Box 297, Woodbridge, N.Y. 12789, or call (914) 434-7580.

Villa Roma Resort and Country Club at Callicoon has 225 rooms and is open the year-round. The cuisine is Italian-American and served on the American Plan. There are indoor/outdoor pools, the same for tennis courts, a health club, nightly entertainment and disco, a children's program and golf. The summer weekly rates are $179-$239 per person, double occupancy. For reservations write Callicoon, New York, 12723 or call toll-free (800) 727-8455.

Wolfe's Maple Breeze Resort has rates of $72 for one person, $128-$163 for two persons, two beds, 7/3-8/21. From 5/25-7/2 and 8/22-10/25, the one-person rate is $63 and two persons, two beds $124-$160. Wolfe's Resort is located five miles south of the junction of State Route 23 and two miles east of State Route 32. No pets. A large number of indoor and outdoor sports are available. For reservations write the resort at 360 Cauterskill Road, 12414, or call (518) 943-3380.

Zucker's Glen Wild Hotel and Country Club has 50 rooms and is open July 1-September 7. It is on the American Plan, is strictly Glatt Kosher, and the club observes the Sabbath. There's an outdoor pool and swimming in Mirror Lake as well as rowboating and fishing. In summer, the weekly rate is $240-$325 per person, double occupancy. On weekends the rate is $90-$140 per person, double occupancy. For reservations write the club at Glen Wild, N.Y. 12738 or call (914) 434-7470.

State Campsites

T he New York State Department of Environmental Conservation provides a few campsites in the Catskills. Unlike private campsites, they don't have electrical hookups. They permit six people in each site, and charge $9 to $15 per night. Each facility provides the following amenities, except as noted: Trailer and/or tent sites, picnicking, trailer dumping station, showers, pond or lake, river or stream, power boats allowed, rowboats/canoes, boat and canoe rentals, boat launching, swimming, bath houses, lifeguards, fishing, hiking.

1. The Beaverkill is off Route 17, seven miles northwest of Livingston Manor. (914) 439-4291. No pond or lake, no boat launching.

2. Mongaup Pond is off Route 17, seven miles northwest of De-Bruce. (914) 439-4233. No power boats allowed.

3. The Kenneth L. Wilson is off Route 28, four miles east of Mt. Tremper on County Route 40. (914) 679-7020. No power boats allowed, no boat and canoe rentals.

4. Woodland Valley, off Route 28, six miles southwest of Phoenicia. (914) 688-7647. No pond or lake, no boat launching, no swimming.

5. Little Pond is off Route 17, 14 miles northwest of Livingston Manor. (914) 439-5480.

6. Bear Spring Mountain is off Route 206, five miles southeast of Walton (607) 865-6989. No showers, no river or stream, no power boats allowed.

7. Devil's Tombstone is on Route 214, four miles south of Hunter (514) 688-7160. No trailer dumping station, no showers, no river or stream, no boat launching, no swimming.

8. North/South Lake is off Route 23A, three miles northeast of Haines Falls. (518) 589-5058. No river or stream and no power boats allowed.

Private Campsites

These campgrounds are privately owned and often have more facilities than state-run campsites. All area codes are 914 unless otherwise noted.

1. Baily Lake Campsite, P.O. Box 127, Kiamesha, N.Y. 12751; 794-0133 or 791-1698. It is three miles north of Monticello off Route 42 on Fraser Road. It is open year-round. A total of 350 acres; 100 sites have electrical hookups and 15 have sewer hookups. There are two dumping stations and all sites have tables and fireplaces. Flush toilets and hot showers are provided. There's an outdoor pavilion on the lake with an indoor lounge, a campstore and a children's play area. You can swim in the lake, fish and rent boats. Hiking trails are available and so are winter sports activities.

2. Birchwood Acres Camping Resort, Box 482, Woodridge, N.Y. 12789; 434-4743. It is open from May 1-October 11. There are 150 acres and 227 sites with electrical hookups, 136 with sewer connections and 227 tables and fireplaces. There are 25 flush toilets, 21 hot showers, a recreation building, children's playground, store, laundry, movies and planned activities. There's a pool and a lake. You can fish, rent boats, play tennis, shuffleboard, baseball, etc. The basic daily fee is $24.50.

3. Butternut Grove Campsite, RD 1, Roscoe, N.Y. 12776; (617) 498-4224. It is seven miles west of Roscoe on Old Route 17 and is open from April 1-December 1. There are 75 sites with electric and water hookups, a dumping station, 75 tables and fireplaces, 12 flush toilets, four hot showers, a children's play area, a laundry room and nearby swimming.

4. Covered Bridge Campsite, 778 Horseshoe Lake Road, Swan Lake, N.Y. 12783; 883-6575. It is on County Road 141. Open from May 15-October 10, it offers 80 sites, 60 with water and electrical hookups, 80 tables and fireplaces, six flush toilets, and hot showers. Its location on Willowemoc Creek assures great fishing and hunting.

5. Happy Days Campground, 778 Horshoe Lake Road, Swan Lake, N.Y. 12783; 583-6575. Paddle boats can be rented along with trailers. It is on County Road 141 and open from May 1-December 10. It offers 30 sites, 15 with electrical hookups, a dumping station, 30 tables and fireplaces, six flush toilets and four hot showers. There's a recreation room, a laundry and a store. The basic daily fee is $14.

6. Hilltop Farm Campsites, Forest Road, P.O. Box 138, Mountaindale, N.Y. 12763; 434-1017. It is open from May 15 to October 15. There are 86 sites with electrical hookups, 45 with sewage, a dumping station, flush toilets and hot showers. They have a recreation building, fireplaces and tables. Paddle boats and trailers can be rented. There's a pool, a store and fishing.

7. Hunter Lake Campground, 177 Hunter Lake Drive, Parksville, New York, 12768; 292-3629. It is open from Memorial Day through September 15. A total of 130 acres on Hunter Lake are open to campers only. There's a dumping station, 90 tables and fireplaces, 10 flush toilets, 10 hot showers, a recreation building, a children's play area, and a store. You can swim and fish in the lake and rental boats are available.

8. Indian Head Canoes & Campground, Route 97, Barryville, N.Y. 12719; (800) 874-BOAT or 557-8777. It is two miles north of Barryville on Route 97, and is open April 22-October 8. There are hot showers, flush toilets, tent sites, fireplaces and picnic tables. Excellent fishing and canoeing on the Delaware River.

9. Jerry's Three River Campground, P.O. Box 7, Pond Eddy, New York, 12770; 557-6078. It has 39 acres, on which are 62 sites for seasonal or overnight RV sites with electric/water and dumping services. There are 12 flush toilets, eight hot showers, 62 tables and fireplaces, a camp store and restaurant. For recreation, there are facilities for volleyball, softball, canoeing, rafting and fishing.

10. Jubilee Camplands, Box 173, Ferndale, N.Y. 12734; 292-8500. In the off-season call 279-9383. Take Exit 101 off Route 17, then drive two miles to Deveny Road. There are 35 campsites, 20 with full hookups and seven with electricity only. Camplands furnishes a dumping station, flush toilets, hot showers and tables. There's a pool, a children's play area, a recreation building and a store.

11. Kittatinny Campgrounds, P.O. Box 95, Barryville, N.Y. 12719; (800) FLOAT-KC, 557-8611 or 557-8004. This is river front camping plus canoe, water raft, kayak and tube trips. With 250 natural acres and a stocked trout stream, it has wooded sites. There's a camp store, a delicatessen, a pool, pavilion, arcade and showers. There's free camping for non-profit groups. It is two miles north of Barryville on Route 97 and it is open April-October.

12. Koinonia Campgrounds, 165 Lake View Drive, Highland Lake, New York, 12743; 557-8335. From Port Jervis, take route 97N to Barryville's Route 55E, drive four miles from the Delaware River to the campgrounds. There are 40 large wooded sites with electrical hook-ups, water, showers and a laundry. You can fish and swim in the lake and take trips on the Delaware River. There are also cabins and trailers for rent.

13. Lazy "G" Campground and Cottages, Box 563, Woodbridge, N.Y. 12789; 434-3390. From Route 17, take Exit 109, make a right turn and then a left turn on Glen Wild Road, another left at the first light, and a right onto Greenfield Road. It is open May 15-October 1. There are 30 sites on its 27 acres with electrical hookups, 30 with sewage connections and a dumping station. There are 50 tables and fireplaces and the basic daily fee is $18. In addition, there are 12 flush toilets, six hot showers, a recreation building, adult lounges, a play area, a store, pool, pond and fishing.

14. Miller Hollow Campground, RFD 3, Route 30, Roscoe, N.Y. 12776; (617) 363-7492. It is on Pepacton Reservoir and open April 1-October 15 and during the hunting season October 15-December 15. The 50 sites are on 68 acres, 40 with electrical hookups and a dumping station. There are 50 tables and fireplaces and the basic daily fee is $14. Six flush toilets, six hot showers, a play area, a store, bait shop, laundry and bottled gas are also available.

Hunting

In the Catskills there are more than a quarter of a million acres of steep, rugged public land. Most of it is woodland. There are a number of landowner-cooperative hunting areas on private lands that charge fees. The Catskills provide excellent hunting for grouse, squirrel, woodcock and turkey, with limited numbers of cottontail rabbits.

Wild turkeys disappeared from New York State in the mid-1800s due to over-hunting. They did not reappear until a few years ago, when intensive management of the species and changing land use made it possible for their return in large numbers.

The spring bearded turkey hunt is open most of the month of May in the Catskills, and a second tom may be taken in the last half of the season. This season opens a half-hour before sunrise and closes every day at noon so bring your fishing rod to try your luck with trout, pike and panfish angling as well.

The October-November turkey season in the Catskills allows turkeys of any age or sex to be taken. Gray squirrels and ruffled grouse usually inhabit the same areas as turkeys so your choice of game is covered by the same small game license.

Wild turkeys can be elusive and you must take several precautions in hunting them. Camouflage is a must since a turkey can detect the slightest movement and sees everything in color even if you wear standard clothing that includes a camouflage cap, headnet, jacket, pants and even gloves! No matter how carefully you walk through the woods you will find it virtually impossible to get close enough to a turkey for a shot unless you use a turkey call. It's a must, and you should master its use before you hunt. Used in the springtime the gadget imitates the sound of a hen looking for a mate. For those who have mastered the device, a lusting gobbling will be the response from any tom within earshot. The more seductive you make your call, the better chance you'll have of getting a shot. In the fall, your call attempts to imitate one of a family flock that is regrouping after being separated.

Once you are within range it is imperative to take your time and shoot carefully in order to hit the bird's neck and head. A body shot will only cripple the turkey and it will escape. The Catskill region is less heavily hunted for turkeys than the rest of the state so your chances are improved.

Big Game Hunting

In New York State's two major hunting zones, called simply the northern and southern zones, big-game hunting conditions vary widely and each has different regulations.

Over 700,000 New York residents buy big game licenses, and three-quarters of them hunt in the southern zone, which includes the Catskills. This zone has areas of high intensity farming as well as vast sections of rolling, rugged topography in bushland, young forest and valley farmland. Deer levels are higher in the southern zone because of the better quality of the range and milder winter weather. The deer in most of this zone are intensively managed through a quota system, permitting the taking of antlerless deer as well as buck. Permits to take antlerless deer are issued in pre-determined numbers, based on the number of deer to be removed in each Deer Management Unit. There's no quota system for legal buck hunting (deer with antlers three inches or longer) and by the end of the hunting season nearly 75% of the legal bucks are removed.

Licenses

Licenses and most regulations for hunting big game in the Catskills are the same as for the Adirondacks. Therefore, only the differences will be noted.

The archery seasons for deer and bear are from October 15 through November 20 and December 14-18. Sunday hunting is allowed and deer of either sex may be taken. The regular deer season is from November 21 through December 13, and for bear November 26 through December 31. The muzzle-loading season is December 14-20. Only bucks can be taken and Sunday hunting is allowed.

Black bear can be taken during the archery season November 26-December 13, and December 15-December 19.

All bear taken in the Catskills must be examined by a wildlife biologist before the animal is skinned and prepared for consumption. Further instructions will be provided the hunter when the bear kill is reported on the toll-free telephone number.

Fishing

Small mouth bass, large mouth bass, walleye and pickerel are found throughout the Catskill region. They can be caught with the same lures as those used in the Adirondacks. There are no muskellunge in the Catskills.

Brown trout are the most plentiful in the Catskills, particularly in the reservoirs, where they commonly reach sizes of five to 15 pounds. There are some brook and rainbow trout but this is not a good region for them. Landlocked salmon have not been introduced into this area, except in the Delaware River.

An Experience You'll Never Forget

A 10-day or two-week trip by car through the Adirondacks and Catskills is well within the realm of possibility, and for some people that may be sufficient time to see these regions. But it is humanly impossible to take full advantage of the vast number of things to see and do in that amount of time. If you would like to enjoy these idyllic regions to the fullest, visit the Catskills and the Adirondacks in separate years or lengthen the time and spend it in both of them.

In our modern world where transportation permits travel between states or countries so quickly – one country one day, another country the second day – something vital and important has been lost. One of the great joys of life is to step off the daily treadmill and take the time to rest and relax. It is not only refreshing, invigorating, but absolutely essential to a person's well-being.

Before this book was published I invited my old comrade from World War II, Thomas Robert "Bob" Vaucher (we fought together in the Army Air Forces in World War II, he as a B-29 pilot and me as a bombardier-navigator) to join me in a 10-day automobile trip through the Adirondacks and Catskills. He eagerly accepted. At the time he was 75 years old and I was 79. We had each experienced serious medical problems but, for the most part, we were in good health.

For us this trip was a rejuvenation process and slowly the tired, anxious lines disappeared from our faces as we let nature heal us. We have known so much strife and turmoil in peace and war, but those years were momentarily forgotten as we toured these magnificent forest lands where life is lived more simply.

I hope you'll do likewise, letting nature govern your life for whatever time you can spare. I'm confident a trip to the Adirondacks and the Catskills will be an experience you'll never forget.

Additional Reading

from Hunter Publishing

BATTLEFIELDS OF THE CIVIL WAR 1:
A GUIDE FOR TRAVELLERS
$11.95, ISBN 1-55650-603-1, 310pp

"For each battlefield, combat descriptions are keyed to a map, so that with book in hand you can pinpoint the action. Fortunately, Mr. Howard is no retailer of dry facts; his accounts of battle are fast-paced and riveting. He also gives information on accommodations, dining, and sightseeing in each area." Passport Newsletter.

This, the first book of the series, covers in depth the battles of 1st and 2nd Manassas, Shiloh, Antietam, Gettysburg, Vicksburg, Chicamauga, Ft. Donelson, Stones River, Fredericksburg, and Lookout Mountain. You will find here both the story of the battles themselves and a fieldguide to touring the battlefields today.

THE GREAT AMERICAN WILDERNESS:
TOURING AMERICA'S NATIONAL PARKS
$11.95, ISBN 1-55650-567-1, 320pp

The 41 most scenic parks throughout the US including Acadia, the Great Smokey Mountains, Yellowstone, Hawaii Volcanoes, the Grand Canyon, Big Bend, the Everglades and many more. This tells you where to stay, where to eat, which roads are most crowded or most beautiful, how much time to allow, what you can safely skip and what you must not miss. Detailed maps of each park show all the surrounding access routes and special sections tell you how to make the most of your time if you only have a couple of hours.

WHERE TO STAY IN NEW ENGLAND
$11.95, ISBN 1-55650-602-3, 512pp

"... isn't just your usual B&B or hotel listing, but a selection of almost all hotels, motels, country houses, condos and cottages for rent in the region.... Highly recommended: much more comprehensive in scope than competitors." Reviewer's Bookwatch.

Over 5,000 places are listed in this all-inclusive guide. Brief descriptions are supplemented by address, phone number (toll-free when available) and prices. Special sections are dedicated to chain hotels and deals they offer to business travellers, school groups, government workers and senior citizens.

Other guides in the **Where to Stay** *series:*

AMERICA'S EASTERN CITIES $11.95, ISBN 1-55650-600-7, 416pp
AMERICA'S WESTERN CITIES $11.95, ISBN 1-55650-420-9, 416pp
MID-ATLANTIC STATES $12.95, ISBN 1-55650-631-7, 446pp
AMERICA'S HEARTLAND $13.93, ISBN 1-55650-632-5, 572pp
SOUTHERN CALIFORNIA $12.95, ISBN 1-55650-573-6, 394pp
NORTHERN CALIFORNIA $12.95, ISBN 1-55650-572-8, 280pp
AMERICAN NORTHWEST $12.95, ISBN 1-55650-683-X, 320pp
FLORIDA $12.95, ISBN 1-55650-682-1, 384pp
AMERICAN SOUTHEAST $12.95, ISBN 1-55650-651-1, 500pp
AMERICAN SOUTHWEST $12.95, ISBN 1-55650-652-X, 450pp

All of these titles plus thousands more are available from Hunter Publishing. To receive our free color catalog or to find out more about our books and maps, contact Hunter Publishing, 300 Raritan Center Parkway, Edison NJ 08818, or call (908) 225 1900.